THEMES
for early years

COLOURS

MAX de BÓO

THEMES
for early years

Author Max de Bóo

Editor Irene Goodacre

Series designer Lynne Joesbury

Designers Clare Brewer, Toby Long

Illustrations Cathy Baxter

Cover based on an illustration by Sue Coney

Action Rhymes, Poems and Stories compiled by Jill Bennett

Songs compiled by Peter Morrell

Assemblies chapter by Lesley Prior

with grateful thanks to Madeleine

Designed using Aldus Pagemaker

Published by Scholastic Limited, Villiers House, Clarendon Avenue, Leamington Spa, Warwickshire CV32 5PR

© 1995 Scholastic Limited   Text © 1995 Max de Bóo
7 8 9 0   0 1 2 3 4

The publishers gratefully acknowledge permission to reproduce the following copyright material:
© 1995 Clive Barnwell for 'Burn, candle burn', 'Middle of the ring' and 'My door's a red door'; © 1995 Colin J. Bennett for 'Give us back the night'; © 1995 Pie Corbett for 'I like colours'; © 1989 John Foster for 'Overnight' first published in *Language in Colour* edited by Moira Andrew (1989, Belair); © 1995 Lesley Funge for 'A rainbow world'; © 1995 Ian R. Henderson-Begg for 'Green green green' and 'Up above, down below'; © 1995 Wes Magee for 'In Gran's jewellery box', 'In the church' and 'The autumn leaves'; © 1995 Trevor Millum for 'Colour splash' (words only); © 1992 Tony Mitton for 'Fingerpaints'; © 1995 Peter Morrell for 'A chameleon has no stripes' and 'Can you taste the colour'; © 1988 Judith Nicholls for 'Green song' from *Popcorn Pie* (1988, Mary Glasgow); © 1995 Judith Nicholls for 'Face painting', 'What's yellow then?' and 'Winter morning'; © 1995 Gillian Parker for 'Colour splash' (music only); Penguin Books Limited for 'My window-box' and 'Painting' from *One Blue Boat* by Linda Hammond (1991, Viking Children's Books); Random House UK Limited for 'Colour counting' and 'Roy, the Hat Boy' from *What Shall We Do Today* by Delphine Evans (1985, Hutchinson Children's Books); Reed Consumer Books for 'Sarah and the red things' from *Specially Sarah* by Mary Hoffman (1987, Methuen Children's Books) and 'Tail of a peacock' from *Summer in Small Street* by Geraldine Kaye (1989, Methuen Children's Books); © 1983 Iain Crichton Smith for 'The rainbow' from *A Scottish Poetry Book* edited by A. Bold (1983, Oxford University Press); Stoddart Publishing Company Limited for 'Sun, Sun' from *Don't Eat Spiders* by Robert Heidbreder (Stoddart Publishing).
Every effort has been made to trace copyright holders and the publishers apologise for any inadvertent omissions.

British Library Cataloguing-in-Publication Data A catalogue record for this book is available from the British Library.

ISBN 0-590-53348-7

THEMES
for early years

CONTENTS

INTRODUCTION

In the middle of a sorting game with foods and non-foods, Christopher suddenly exclaimed, 'Do you know what? If you eat dog-food you'll turn into a dog!'

Learning is a curious business. Young children are constantly absorbing a variety of information from the strange new world around them. Ideas are retained in their heads waiting for a situation when information they already have can be linked to something new. In doing so, children often create their own form of reality but, gradually, their ideas become more accurate and coherent until they have the full range of skills and knowledge they will need for adult life.

Two things are very clear. The first is that children need stimulating and varied practical experiences in the early years if they are to acquire the ideas and information they will use in later life. Secondly, although learning can be guided it is rarely acquired in a structured, linear way. Young children learn what is interesting, important or significant to them at that time.

Educators cannot guarantee precisely *what* children will learn, but they can provide a stimulating learning environment that offers experience across the whole curriculum, and which, at the same time, encourages motor and social skills, and increases individual self-esteem.

COLOURS

Why choose the theme of Colours?

First, imagine a world without any colour — picture the twilight world between the end of the day and darkness, a black and white television picture, or dull photocopies of a tulip, fireworks or a beautiful painting.

Our world is full of colour, and the colours offer information as well as pleasure. We use the colour of the cheeks or the tongue to assess the condition of a sick child. We use colour to assess the health of the plants in our gardens, and the ripeness of the fruit in the supermarket. We use colour to identify *our* bus or car and *our* coat on the rack. We choose a skirt, a shirt and the sheets for our bed by the blend of colours that appeal to us. We stop at a red light and go with green. Human sight is a miracle of nature — the human eye can perceive over 2,000 different shades, tones and mixtures of colours.

Colour plays an enormous part in every aspect of human life. Children will be keen to explore and identify its many uses.

HOW TO USE THIS BOOK

This book has been designed to provide early years educators with all the practical ideas and resources needed to work through the theme of Colours.

The following information is designed to help you find your way around the different sections of the book.

TOPIC WEB

The Topic Web on pages 8 and 9 shows how all the activities relate to both the National Curriculum and the Scottish 5–14 Guidelines. You may photocopy these pages to help you plan your theme.

THE ACTIVITY CHAPTERS

The themes of the activity chapters (pages 11–58) are chosen for their relevance to the everyday life of young children and their expanding world. Children learn best when they are in a familiar setting and their ability to see patterns and make generalisations about objects, behaviour and so on, will develop and improve with experience.

Each activity has the following headings:

Objective

The activities in this book are intended for children aged three to six who will have started, or be preparing for primary school. Each activity opens with an objective which focuses on one area of the curriculum, and gives clear learning targets. Many activities will also encourage learning in other parts of the curriculum.

All the activities are practical, requiring co-operative involvement and/or individual work. This provides opportunities for motor and social skills to develop, and the growth of self-esteem.

Group size

Children learn more productively if they are involved in picking out the ideas they will later develop in the hands-on section of the activity. It will often be appropriate to introduce the activity to the group as a whole, then allow the children to work in small groups with regular adult support (for example, help with cutting or writing).

What you need

Very young children have an immense curiosity and hunger for learning. They therefore require a wide range of materials and equipment to stimulate this. Each activity lists the resources required, with the emphasis on items that are readily available or can be obtained in advance. Any books mentioned in the text will also be listed with other recommended materials on page 96.

Preparation

The preparation section simply highlights the things that either you, or you and the children, will need to do before you start the main activity. Preparation speeds up the actual activity and avoids the danger of children becoming bored, or frustrated.

What to do

This section suggests a variety of ways in which the children's interest can be focused on the learning objectives. The practical hands-on part has been kept straightforward and informative.

Discussion

In this section questions are suggested which should stimulate thinking about the subject and related areas. Background information is also given and any possible areas of concern are mentioned here.

Follow-up activities

Some of the suggestions here will reinforce the learning that has come from the activity itself. Other suggestions are offered which extend the ideas in an appropriate cross-curricular way. The main activities, together with the follow-up suggestions, offer a broadly balanced approach to the whole curriculum.

THE DISPLAYS CHAPTER

Displays form an important part of any early years environment, surrounding the children with colour, texture and shape, interesting objects, familiar materials and equipment, and symbolic representation in words, numbers, charts and drawings. The chapter on displays (pages 59–63) is intended to support this and provides ideas for attractive and appropriate displays of the children's work.

THE ASSEMBLIES CHAPTER

This chapter (pages 64–66) offers suggestions for simple assemblies or group sharing-times based on the theme of Colours.

RESOURCES SECTION

You may photocopy all the pages in this section.

Action rhymes and poems, stories and songs

These resources (pages 67–87) have been specially selected to support the theme of Colours. They can be used in a variety of learning situations but are also referred to in the main activities and follow-up suggestions wherever appropriate.

Activity sheets

These sheets (pages 88–95) offer support to the main and follow-up activities. The text suggests ways in which the pages might be used — for example, they could be coloured in and cut out by the children with or without adult help, traced to make cardboard templates, and used as stimuli for questions and discussion.

Recommended materials

Page 96 lists books and other resources that you will find useful for your Colours theme.

EXPRESSIVE ARTS

Planning towards the National Curriculum and the Scottish 5–14 National Guidelines

PREPARING FOR PRIMARY SCHOOL

THE NATIONAL CURRICULUM

The National Curriculum for England and Wales specifies those areas and aspects of the curriculum which should be taught to children in State schools between the ages of five and sixteen. It is not compulsory for children in pre-school education or in independent schools, although many educators in these sectors select material for their teaching programmes from within the National Curriculum.

The 'core' subjects in the National Curriculum are English, mathematics and science, with history, geography, design and technology, information technology, art, music, physical education and religious education making up the remainder.

The National Curriculum provides a Programme of Study for each subject, and asks teachers to assess the level of attainment of each child in the country when they reach Year Two (age six to seven), partly by the use of nation-wide tests, but mostly by asking teachers to use their professional judgement to allocate an overall level to each child.

This book has selected appropriate activities to support or encourage children's learning whether they are bound by the National Curriculum or not. The intention is to provide a broad foundation of learning experiences, from three to six years, that are child-relevant rather than curriculum-driven. Stimulating 'play' or exploration, with all the implications for the development of social and motor control, is given particular emphasis.

Each activity in the book is focused on a particular aspect of learning to support your planning. The Topic Web on pages 8 and 9 shows how each activity in the book relates to a different subject area.

THE SCOTTISH 5–14 NATIONAL GUIDELINES

In Scotland there are National Guidelines for schools on what should be taught to children between the ages of five and fourteen.

These National Guidelines are divided into six main curriculum areas: English language, Mathematics, Environmental studies, Expressive arts, Religious and moral education, Personal and social development.

Within these main areas further subjects are found, for example 'Expressive arts' includes art and design, drama, music and PE. Strands are also identified within each subject, for example Maths includes problem-solving and enquiry, and shape, position and movement.

Most nurseries and playgroups will find that the experiences they are offering children will be laying a good foundation for this curriculum. This book provides activities which have been specially written to prepare for many aspects of it and they will also fit well into the pre-five curriculum guidelines issued by local authorities throughout Scotland.

To help you with your planning, the individual activities have been allocated to separate areas of the curriculum on the Topic Web on pages 8 and 9. The children's personal and social development is an on-going theme that is incorporated throughout the activities in the book.

CHAPTER 1
PEOPLE

This chapter encourages observation of personal characteristics and self-esteem. Feelings, likes and dislikes are explored and valued.

COLOURS ALL AROUND

Objective

English — To use colours as adjectives and create poems.

Group size

Introduce to the whole group, work with four to six children for the writing.

What you need

My Little Book of Colours by Jan Ormerod, the poem, 'I like colours' in the resources section on page 69, objects with very clear colours, including some of your own favourite objects, like a brown teddy, a red mug, yellow buttercups, also a stapler or string, sugar paper and a felt-tipped pen.

Preparation

Make a large wall list of colour words written in colours beside blocks of appropriate colour – red, orange, and so on (see below).

yellow	☐
pink	☐
red	☐
blue	☐
... etc	

Make a 'Floor Book' with large pieces of sugar paper, stapled or tied (for group composition).

Bring a few of your favourite coloured objects into school to show (or ask the children to bring in one or two of their own favourite coloured things).

What to do

Read 'I like colours' – twice through, or read *My Little Book of Colours* in which each colour has a two-page spread with a little boy's clothes and other objects. Show the children your favourite objects and explain that one of the reasons you like them is their colour. Discuss the things they like (or don't like) because of their colour. Use the colour word list to say the words together slowly, enjoying the sounds – 'b..l..u..e', *'yellow'*, **'black!'**.

Write group (or individual) poems about colours, in the Floor Book or elsewhere, for example:
'I like my turquoise teddy
I like my new blue coat
I like eating red apples
I like our marmalade cat
And I like my tongue going purple
when I eat loads of blackberries'
(this is an original poem dictated by children, with the teacher writing).

Discussion

Simple poems can be made by repeating the colour names – 'red, red, red' and 'black, black, black'. Rhythm and rhyme have a big influence on reading development.

Follow-up activities

✧ Decorate the poems in the Floor Book or let the children write out and choose the colour for card-mounting their own poems.
✧ Word-process and print out the poems.
✧ At story-time read out the children's poems – or encourage them to do this themselves.
✧ Give tongue-twisters like 'red lorry, yellow lorry' or 'red leather, yellow leather'.
✧ Read *Green Eggs and Ham* by Dr Seuss, in which a character keeps refusing to eat green eggs and ham, but gives in eventually to find that he actually likes them!
✧ Make a chart of the children's favourite colours.

MY COLOUR – YOUR COLOUR

Objective

Mathematics – To use personal characteristics to encourage counting and number recognition.

Group size

Four to six children.

What you need

Plain buff-coloured card, crayons (pastels, chinagraph pencils, or felt-tipped pens), scissors, large dice, mirrors (large plastic type).

Preparation

Cut two pieces of card (roughly A4) for each child. Write out the numbering system for the mathematical game on a piece of card (with numerals or words alongside) as follows:

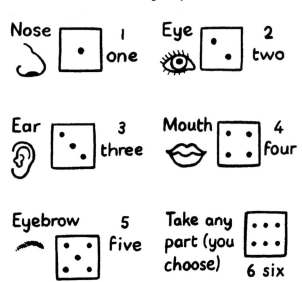

Prepare a simple, uncoloured version of the game with a cardboard face shape and cut out eyes, nose, ears, etc.

What to do

Look into a mirror and ask the children to describe what they think you can see – face and features. Give them mirrors to describe the colour of their own hair, mouth, eyes, skin, and the shape of their nose and face.

Show the children the sample game and the dice and ask them to draw two big faces on their own cards. On one, they should colour the face shape only, on the other they should draw and colour in all the features, then cut them out. Explain that the dice is thrown to win eyes, ears, and so on to put on to the empty face. Each child uses her or his own face and features in the game and the first child to complete the face is the winner.

Discussion

Ask the children what colour of crayon they will use for their skin and their hair. Accept their choice of colour and use any unusual selections as a point for discussion. Ask about the shape of their face. How many times will they need to throw a one? a three? What happens if they throw a six?

Follow-up activities

✧ Ask the children to make alternative features – a sad mouth, or a shouting one, great big eyes, frowning eyebrows, or curly hair. Laminate the faces and features for future use.
✧ Compare the children's face shapes with squares, circles and ovals.
✧ Set up the painting area with very bright colours. Ask the group to imagine and paint the face of a big bad giant, or a visitor from outer space, or a circus clown.
✧ Use the children's eye and hair colour choices to make sets and charts.

Green eyes	Blue eyes	Brown eyes	Hazel eyes
Mai Lily	Maria Jimmy	Brian Sit Yin	Sarah

✧ Read the poem 'Face painting' in the resources section, page 72.
✧ Read 'My naughty little sister and the twins' in *When My Naughty Little Sister Was Good* by Dorothy Edwards (Mammoth) where she confuses twins with mirror images!
✧ Learn the song 'You're smiling' in the Scholastic Collections book, *Songs*.

COLOURS FROM LONG AGO

Objective

History – To develop an awareness of how things change over time by comparing dyes, ancient and modern.

Group size

Introduce to all, but work with four to six children when dyeing.

What you need

Old white cotton (or cotton and polyester) sheets or shirts, access to an electric kettle, three or four different vegetables and spices such as onion skins, turmeric, blackberries, beetroot, carrots; non-staining dishes or bowls, potatoes, two or three cold water dyes, perhaps bright red and blue or vivid green, salt, two or three plastic buckets or bowls, washing line and pegs, rubber gloves, spaghetti tongs or wooden spoons, elastic bands, string, newspaper to cover the table, an old photograph of family or friends.

Preparation

Tear up the cotton cloth into enough squares for every child to have two pieces, with a few spares. Name them with a non-soluble pen.

What to do

Show the children the old photograph and explain that long ago people could not buy dyes in the shops like today, and had to use things they had to hand. Encourage the children to suggest what those things might be. Show the potato and carrots and discuss what effect these might have on the white cloth.

Prepare vegetable dyes by adding half a cup of hot water to crushed berries or beetroot, onion skins, grated carrots or turmeric. Each child then chooses a colour to dip, or potato print one of their squares and hangs it up to dry. Later, mix cold water dyes with salt in the buckets as instructed on the dye packet. Tie string or rubber bands around other cloths, reinforcing the children's tying. Steep the tied cloths in the dye for half an hour, then remove and dry with the ties intact before removing the tie bands. Open out and compare the results of the vegetable dyes with those of the commercial ones.

Discussion

Ask the children to predict the outcomes, then describe the results. Can they suggest why some parts of the cloth stayed white?

Follow-up activities

✧ Display the children's tie-dyed cloths on the washing line across the room or splayed out in a wall-mounted fan shape.
✧ Make a display of photographs of either the children today and as babies, or the children, their parents or guardians and grandparents.
✧ Collect and display clothes – baby, child, adult or old-fashioned and modern. Put some in the home corner for role play.
✧ Visit a museum, local statues, an art gallery or church with engraved brasses, and look at the clothes.
✧ Teach the children to sing 'Middle of the ring' on page 86 and 'A rainbow world' on page 87 of the resources section.

COLOURED STATUES

Objective

PE – To encourage listening and responding, and the development of co-ordinated movements.

Group size

The whole group.

What you need

Enough space to move around freely. Equal numbers of coloured PE bands or crêpe-paper bands, a cassette recorder and cassette of pleasant music.

Preparation

Make comfortable crêpe-paper bands if needed, to go over the shoulder and down to the waist.

What to do

Warm up for the lesson by playing 'Statues' with the emphasis on Colour. Ask each child to choose a coloured band, then call out one colour at a time. The children whose colour is called freeze, while the other children continue to run (or skip) quietly in and out until their colour is called. When all the children are 'frozen' reverse the process. Play the game two or three times, calling quietly to encourage listening. Children who fail to freeze can sit down on the floor for that game period.

Continue to emphasise the listening and moving skills in the following colour game. Again use the coloured bands, but this time the children are to become plants spaced about in a garden. Explain that the children are to grow tall when they hear their colour.

Choose various coloured plants which are familiar, for example yellow buttercups, green holly, red poppies, bluebells and so on. From time to time say 'flowers bright' in a verse for all the children to grow together.

Verse 1
'I have a little garden, where I like to go,
Watch all the colours and see them grow.'
(Children crouch down)

Verse 2
'Roses red, roses red, grow so tall,
(Children grow and stretch up)
Then the Autumn winds blow
(Children sway)
And down... they... fall.'
(Speak softly to encourage controlled 'falling'.)
Verses 3, 4, 5 then go – 'Berries blue...', 'Tulips yellow...', 'Flowers bright'.
Finish by playing Coloured Statues again.

Discussion

Some of the flowers can be more than one colour, for example, roses and tulips. Berries can be blue, purple or red, so a little licence is needed for which plants 'grow tall' or 'fall'. Let the children suggest and show how each colour might move. White on tiptoe? Green waving up and down? Red flickering and spiky? Gold slow and heavy?

Follow-up activities

✧ The most important follow-up here is to repeat the games and movements on other occasions, to reinforce the importance of a safe, listening atmosphere when doing movement lessons or PE.
✧ A 'showing' Assembly could provide an opportunity for the children to show their skills in listening and responding. If space and time allow show Coloured Statues *and* the Garden game, or just the latter.
✧ Say the action rhyme 'My window-box', on page 68 of the resources section.

TREASURE CHEST

❋ ❋

Objective

Design and Technology — To use colour as the main design feature when making classroom 'jewellery'.

Group size

Groups of four to six.

What you need

Materials for colouring and threading such as milk bottle tops, beads, short lengths of coloured straws, cotton reels, foil-wrapped pieces of cardboard tubing, macaroni; smooth string, laces and shearing elastic or large blunt darning needles and thick cotton thread, also bead-making materials such as dough or clay, wooden or plastic piercing tools, paints, a collection of old, inexpensive jewellery (from charity shops, or your own), a 'jewellery' box.

Preparation

Create a 'treasure chest' with a large jewellery box, or a biscuit tin lined with foil or lurex cloth. Fill it to overflowing with the beads and bracelets, rings and necklaces, anklets and brooches. Check all safety catches and fasten them tight or remove them. Make threading holes where required. Cut different lengths of string or shearing elastic. Dip macaroni in a cupful of water with added food colouring and dry on paper.

What to do

Display the treasure chest with the open lid and the jewels tumbling over the sides. Let the children handle the jewels and describe their colour and

pattern. Ask the children to suggest where on the body the jewels might be worn, who might have owned them long ago and any other stories about the pretend lost treasure chest.

Make some jewellery, stringing beads and buttons, rolling and piercing clay beads, and painting where needed or desired. Give free colour choice for the first jewel but ask the children to choose materials in just two or three colours for their second one.

Discussion

Ask the children why people like to wear jewels. How many reasons can they think of (looking handsome, pretty, important, belonging...)? Ask them to measure the strings around their necks and wrists for fitting — allow an extra 10cm to be safe! Discuss what might happen if the clay beads are strung next to the cardboard tube pieces or the cotton reel next to the macaroni.

Follow-up activities

✦ Read and count with the poem 'In Gran's jewellery box', on page 68.
✦ Look at the fastenings on the jewellery and make a collection of fastenings.
✦ Do motor-skill reinforcement work with lacing cards and shoelaces.
✦ Put out some metals and non-metals on a testing table with magnets.

AWAY FROM HOME

Objective

Geography — To develop the children's awareness of their own locality in a mapping exercise.

Group size

Ten to twelve children.

What you need

The activity sheet on page 88, pencils, colouring pencils, *Moving Molly* by Shirley Hughes (Red Fox).

Preparation

Photocopy a map for each child, and one spare copy, mounted on card (preferably enlarged).

What to do

Tell a story about when you last moved home, or read *Moving Molly*, a story about a little girl who leaves her first home in a busy basement flat and goes to live in a quiet house in the country. Then use the following poem for further discussion:

Granny's house is green and brown
Aunt Mabel's house is pink
And Ben's blue house is near the town
But mine is best I think.

My uncle's home is red and grey
My school is white and black
And Sally's home is far away
But mine is near the park.

Discuss the colours of the building you are in and the children's homes (the bricks, stone or paint). Show the children the card-mounted map and take your fingers for a walk. Ask them to tell you how

to get to the school, the park or the bus-stop, without crossing over the lines.

Explain that they can colour in the houses and flats on their own maps and draw lines from their 'map' home to their friends' houses, the park and so on. The children can draw in other buildings on the map or draw them elsewhere, then colour them, cut them out and paste them on.

Discussion

Encourage the children to talk about their experiences of moving home — themselves or friends or a parent — and 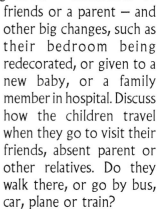 other big changes, such as their bedroom being redecorated, or given to a new baby, or a family member in hospital. Discuss how the children travel when they go to visit their friends, absent parent or other relatives. Do they walk there, or go by bus, car, plane or train?

Follow-up activities

✧ Ask the children to draw, colour and cut out their homes and stick them on to the large map; display this and use it for discussion.

✧ Use (perhaps laminated) the large map for play with toy cars and people (plastic or made with modelling clay).

✧ Make changes in the home corner — you could paint the cot or hang up a new 'picture'. Add two or three small suitcases for packing the soft toys' clothes so that they can move or go travelling.

✧ Read *I Don't Want to* by Sally Grindley (Methuen), about a little boy's first day at school.

✧ Make a 'feely map' with straight and bendy straws stuck on to card for the paths, and different pieces of fabric for a silky 'pond', a rough tweedy 'field' or a prickly teasel bush.

✧ Write letters to an absent parent, someone in hospital, or a friend who has moved.

✧ Play robot movement games in PE, giving commands such as 'Forward three steps', 'Turn left' and so on.

BIRTHDAY FESTIVAL FLOAT

Objective

History – To encourage children's awareness of the passage of time and the meaning of 'yesterday, today and tomorrow'.

Group size

Introduce to the whole group, but do the decorating with four to six children.

What you need

Kipper's Birthday by Mick Inkpen (Hodder & Stoughton), a sturdy trolley (which can take the weight of a child), smaller trolleys or prams for carrying toys, crêpe and tissue paper, balloon pump and balloons, foil and coloured foil paper, masking tape, card, pencils and colouring pens or crayons, a large calendar.

Preparation

Check that the trolley is strong enough to bear the weight of a child in the group. Cut the crêpe and tissue paper into long strips.

What to do

Read *Kipper's Birthday* through twice. Kipper prepares for his birthday by making a cake and decorations but forgets to deliver the invitations until the day of his birthday and is disappointed when none of his friends come. They come the following day as the invitations said 'Come tomorrow'.

Use the big calendar to identify a date and a day of the week. What day was yesterday? What day will tomorrow be?

Show the children the trolleys to decorate for a birthday parade for people and toys. Choose some of the children to begin decorating the different festival floats – winding paper around the handles, tying on balloons and streamers and any other form of decoration they care to attempt. Each float could be a different combination of colours – red, green and gold or blue, yellow and silver. If it is dry outside, parade the floats, with the non-pushers or riders playing percussion instruments or whistles at a safe distance.

Discussion

Ask the children to remember their last birthday. Did anyone have a party and invite friends? How did their friends know when to go to the party?

Remind the children that the decorations have to be colourful but not get in the way of the wheels or the passengers. Ask the children to choose clothes for the toys or themselves to wear for their turn in the float.

Follow-up activities

✧ Take photographs of the parade and display these for parents and other people to see.
✧ Read 'Roy, the hat boy' on page 76 of the resources section.
✧ Write out copying cards for invitations saying 'Please come to my birthday party tomorrow at 12 o'clock. Don't be late. Love, ...'. Use them again to ask the children 'What day is tomorrow?' What day was yesterday?'
✧ Make a time-line or calendar with the children's birthday dates marked clearly along it. Let the children colour and cut out their face and write the name to go with it.
✧ Let the children make sets of their friends' ages compared with their own.

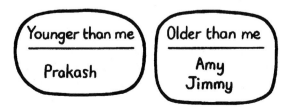

CHILDREN'S FESTIVALS

Objective

RE – To show how faiths and religions place a high value on children.

Group size

Introduce to the whole group, but work with four to six children when making and displaying.

What you need

A Japanese adult (perhaps a parent or neighbour) willing to come and talk, a kimono or a picture of traditional Japanese dress, dolls and soft toys – your own and classroom ones, bamboo garden canes, card, red and gold felt-tipped pens or shiny foil, red paint, scissors, a selection of grocery or shoeboxes, cereal packets, glue sticks or adhesive.

Preparation

Ask the children to bring their favourite doll or soft toy to the group. Make two or three cardboard templates of a large A4 carp fish or cut out several fish for colouring and sticking. Decorate one of these in red and gold on one side. Make a display space with shelves or boxes covered with cloths or coloured paper.

What to do

Ask your Japanese visitor to describe what happens during the Japanese children's festivals and wear or show the kimono or display the picture. (Traditional kimonos are worn by both men and women.)

If you have not found a Japanese adult to help with this activity, try to create a Japanese atmosphere with posters, pictures in books and so on. Explain that at Hina-Matsuri all girls in the family celebrate and make a special display of dolls in colourful clothes.

Discuss the boys' festival, Tango-no-seku, when boys are reminded to grow up like the carp fish which is big and strong, bright and colourful. Pictures of carp are stuck on to the tops of bamboo sticks to celebrate this festival.

Show the coloured carp you have prepared and ask the children to suggest other ways of colouring the carp red and gold.

Then let the children colour and decorate the carp fish and fasten them on to lengths of cane. Set up the display of dolls and soft toys.

Discussion

The Shinto religion celebrates children in the family on three occasions during the year: Hina-Matsuri, the Girls' or Dolls' Festival; Tango-no-

seku, or the Boys' Festival; and Shichi-go-san when girls aged 7, boys aged 5 and all children aged 3 go to the temple.

Discuss feelings about sisters and brothers, and how our families show their love for us. Ask some of the children to show their dolls and explain why they are so special.

Follow-up activities

✧ Use the carp on canes to make a ritual dance for the Spring Festival, for example, moving like cold winter – falling snow, blowing winds. Children stand in spaces with the bamboo-carp canes while the others dance between them fighting the winter away. Then demonstrate the warm sun, the growing flowers and playful lambs.
✧ Celebrate the arrival of a new doll or toy.
✧ Make sets or charts of brothers and sisters.
✧ Paint pictures of the dolls and toys brought in.
✧ Read 'The Christening' in *When We Were Very Young* by A.A. Milne (Methuen).

CHAPTER 2
ANIMALS

Young children often have contact with a wide range of animals, such as insects, birds and small pets. This chapter focuses on different animal characteristics such as skin colour and camouflage, pattern, shape and movement. The underlying message is that we must show consideration towards all the animals who share our world.

CHAMELEON CAMOUFLAGE

Objective

Science — To look at colour and camouflage in animals.

Group size

All children can join in the introduction and walk, do the colouring activity with four to six children.

What you need

The Mixed-up Chameleon by Eric Carle (Puffin), photocopied pages or card templates of the chameleon (page 89), paints — in different shades of green, and bright colours.

Preparation

Cut out a sample chameleon and paint it in rather lurid colours on one side, greens on the other. Arrange for extra adults to go with you on the walk.

What to do

Read *The Mixed-up Chameleon* — in which a chameleon not only changes colour but his envy of other animals makes him change parts of his body also before he changes back, happily, to himself.

Show your painted chameleon and tell the children she wants to find places nearby where she could hide, in safety. Go out for a short walk, stopping periodically to place the chameleon against a background such as grass, bushes, walls, doors, or tree trunks. When obviously not hidden, ask the children what colours the chameleon needs to be to hide in those places.

Back at your base, let the children colour and cut out chameleons. One side must be painted to hide the chameleon in greenery (grass, bushes, or trees) and the other side can be any colour they choose — for fun, or to help the animal hide in another place. When the chameleons are dry, take the children for a second walk so that they can test their animals against different backgrounds.

Discussion

Can the children guess why real chameleons *do* change colour (to catch flies, to frighten, or avoid being eaten by bigger animals, to find a mate, and so on)?

Discuss the reasons why people would want to be camouflaged, perhaps bird-watchers or soldiers on manoeuvres, *or* seen clearly — think about lollipop people, police and firefighters, even school uniforms.

Follow-up activities

✧ Count the toes on the chameleon's feet.

✧ Read *How to Hide a Butterfly and Other Insects* by Ruth Heller (Kingfisher).

✧ In PE, or at playtime, encourage awareness of balancing in narrow places, like the chameleon — ask the children to walk through spaces between mats without touching them on either side, or along benches, and so on.

✧ Write stories about 'The chameleon who came to visit us' — changing colours to suit.

✧ Sing 'A chameleon has no stripes' on page 84 of the resources section.

THE ELEPHANT'S CHILDREN

Objective

Design and Technology – To encourage exploration and selection of materials and colours to make models of elephants.

Group size

Introduce to all, but make the elephants with groups of four to six children.

What you need

Junk modelling materials – cereal packets, boxes, kitchen roll tubes, card, scissors, black and white paint, glue, sticky tape, string, split pins, balloons, newspaper, wallpaper paste, *The Elephant's Child* from the *Just-So* stories by Rudyard Kipling, picture book version (Alfred Knopf).

Preparation

Cut some of the tubes into three or four pieces. Blow up some of the balloons. Prepare some wallpaper paste.

What to do

Read how the elephant's child, who has a short stubby nose at that time, is spanked by all the grown-up animals when he asks them what the crocodile eats for dinner. He goes to ask the crocodile who lives by the 'great grey-green, greasy Limpopo River, all set about with fever-trees'. He escapes being eaten but the crocodile grabs his nose and in the fight the nose gets very stretched. The elephant's child goes back and uses his new long nose to spank his aunts and uncles who then want a trunk for themselves.

Use the boxes and balloons to make elephants with a part (trunk, ears, tail) that moves (consider using split pins, elastic bands, even string!). Discuss elephant colour and how the children can make it just by using black and white paint.

Discussion

Ask the children to tell you how far they think the trunk can reach. Which other parts of an elephant can move? How do our bodies move? What colour are we – hair, eyes, skin, teeth?

Follow-up activities

◇ Display the models (see page 62).
◇ Play a language guessing game, starting off with a colour characteristic only. The children can guess after each statement but the answer should not be confirmed until four or more characteristics have been given, for example, 'I have brown spots.', 'I am very tall.', 'I have four legs.', 'I have two bony horns.', and so on.
◇ Make some junk-modelling crocodiles.

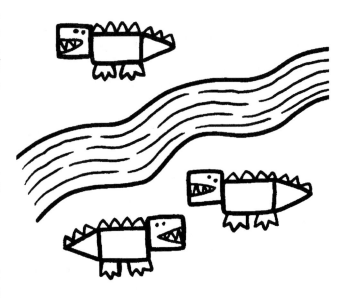

PATCHWORK QUILTS

Objective

Mathematics – To use colour and shape to make and begin to understand patterns.

Group size

Introduce to the whole group but make the patterns with four to six children.

What you need

A patchwork quilt, tea-cosy or printed patchwork fabric, lots of pieces of coloured fabrics, crayons, coloured sticky paper squares, sugar paper or card, scissors, *Elmer* by David McKee (Red Fox).

Preparation

Cut some of the fabrics and sticky paper into regular, equal-sized squares and hexagons. If you have no access to patchwork cloth, make up samples by sticking pieces of fabric on to paper or card in either a hexagon pattern from the centre, or a square pattern in rows.

What to do

Read the story of Elmer, the elephant with patchwork colours instead of elephant grey. Show the patchwork material and tell a patchwork story of your own, recalling real or imaginary origins of the different fabrics and the people who wore the clothes. For example, the material might have come from a faraway country or be part of a giant's lost handkerchief. Look at the fabrics and discuss the colours and patterns in them. Show the children your prepared paper or cloth patterns and the starting point. Ask the children to glue their pieces of fabric, or sticky squares, to make 'round' patterns and 'straight' patterns.

Discussion

Can the children make up different stories about the fabric pieces? What shapes are the pieces? Do any of them know somebody who does patchwork?

Follow-up activities

✧ Make a fabric picture of Elmer, the patchwork elephant or use the Elmer Day colours of the other elephants as a stimulus for patchwork designs.

✧ Ask the children to bring pieces of fabric from home to tell (and write with help) their real or imaginary stories. The fabric can then be used in collages or patchwork.
✧ Explore pattern and tessellation with plane shapes, such as squares, rectangles, triangles, circles, regular pentagons and hexagons.
✧ Go for a walk around some nearby buildings and look for repeat patterns in wall decorations, floor tiles, brickwork, and so on.
✧ Bring flowers and leafy twigs in to show to the group. Leaves usually grow in repeat patterns on stems and some flower petals have repeat patterns.
✧ Use needles and thread with older children to sew patchwork pieces together, back to back, with simple seams.

...NT COLOURS

Objective

English — To encourage recognition of colour words.

Group size

The whole group.

What you need

Elmer by David McKee (Red Fox), the activity sheet on page 90, paints or crayons, scissors, sticky tape.

Preparation

Make photocopies of the elephant for each child, with a few spares. Cut out one elephant (leave uncoloured) and the ear. Write your name in the space indicated. Use sticky tape to fasten the ear in place as a flap so that your name is hidden underneath (see below). The sticky tape (on the inside if possible) forms a hinge so that the ear can flap open or shut.

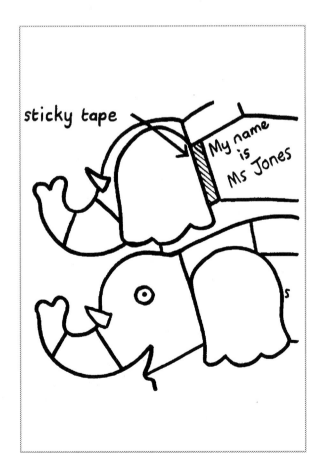

What to do

Read the story of Elmer the multi-coloured patchwork elephant who goes off one day and rolls in some elephant-coloured berries to have the same skin colour as everyone else. When he rejoins the other elephants, no-one recognises him and the elephants are all miserable without their colourful friend. The rain restores Elmer to his own colours to his friends' great delight.

Show the picture of the photocopied patchwork elephant. Ask the children to help you read out the colours on the patches and match the names with the right colours. Discuss the words hidden under the ear flap.

Let the children colour in their photocopied elephants, writing their names in the ear space. Cut out the elephants and the ears, and stick the ear flap in place with a piece of sticky tape on the inside.

Discussion

Ask the children if they can recall the different colours of Elmer's skin. How many colours are there? Did it make the other elephants happy when Elmer had the same skin colour as them? How did the elephants use colour each year on Elmer Day?

Follow-up activities

✧ Mount an extra painted elephant on very thick card and cut along the lines to make a jigsaw.
✧ Use the children's elephants in a display (see page 62).
✧ Sing and move to 'The elephant's song' in *Apusskidu* (A & C Black).
✧ Use grocery boxes and other everyday materials to make a life-sized baby elephant, approximately one metre high. Ask the children what they will use for the legs, the ears, the trunk, and so on.

FINGERMICE

Objective

English – To use mice puppets to stimulate language and drama.

Group size

Introduce to the whole group, but make the puppets and act out the story with between four and six children.

What you need

Mouse Paint by Ellen Stoll Walsh (Orchard), red, yellow and blue paint, brushes, plain white paper, scissors, cardboard or plastic circles (about 12 cm in diameter), strong cotton thread, pink and black felt-tipped pens, glue or glue sticks.

Preparation

Make cat and mouse finger puppets.

The mouse is made from a semi-circle rolled around the mid-point of the straight edge and stuck down into a cone shape (as shown below). This is stuck onto the body, a short cylinder with a tail attached.

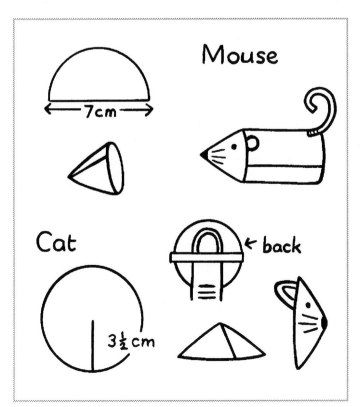

Make the cat with a circle cut once to the centre point, the two cut sides folded under and stuck down in a 'flat' cone shape. Stick a paper strap on behind (see below). Ears can be cut out and stuck on to both animals. Eyes and whiskers can be drawn on or whiskers made with strong thread glued on to the noses.

What to do

Put the fingermouse on your finger and introduce the story of the three clever little mice. *Mouse Paint* tells of three white mice who discover that when their fur is dipped in paint they change colour to red, yellow and blue, and if they are dipped again their colours turn into orange, green, and purple. The mice became white again but remember how to stay camouflaged from the cat.

Let the children draw round, and colour the mice and cat shapes, cut them out and complete the faces. Dramatise the story with the children and their puppets.

Discussion

Ask the children why they think the cat wants to catch mice. What will the mice feel like when the cat is near? What might happen to the cat if she *never* catches any mice and has nothing to eat? What about the farmer who finds the mice eating the wheat grains that are needed to make our bread?

Follow-up activities

✦ Use a modified version of 'This is the house that Jack built':
'This is the room we meet in. This is the bread that lay in the room we meet in. These are the mice that nibbled the bread... etc... This is the cat that chased the mice... This is the dog that barked at the cat... These are the children who stroked the dog... And this is our group!'
✦ Read the poems, 'Colour counting', What's yellow then?' and 'Green Song' on pages 67 and 71 of the resources section.
✦ Play a listening game. A parent mouse (or mice) leaves the room and the children hide with their fingermice. When the parent returns the little mice squeak until they are all found.

BEAUTIFUL BUTTERFLIES

Objective

Art – To use colour in symmetrical patterns.

Group size

Four to six children.

What you need

Acrylic paints (if possible) or poster paint with glue added to a thick runny consistency; sugar paper, card, string, scissors, a place to view caterpillars and butterflies, or *The Very Hungry Caterpillar* by Eric Carle (Picture Puffin).

Preparation

Cut out simple butterfly and moth shapes (butterflies have two pairs of wings, moths have one pair of wings) or fold some sugar paper or card ready to paint.

What to do

Go for a walk to look for butterflies and caterpillars. If this is not possible read *The Very Hungry Caterpillar* in which a little green caterpillar eats his way through various foods from lollipops to chocolate cake, fruit and leaves, until he becomes a butterfly.

Ask the children to describe the colours on the butterfly. Discuss the patterns on each side of the butterfly and explain that this kind of pattern is called 'symmetrical'.

Help the children to paint patterns, folding them immediately and with care, then separating gently to avoid sticking. Use the technique to make butterfly or moth shapes. Use several spoonfuls of the poster paint mixture simultaneously or squeeze out some acrylic paint colours very close to the fold. After folding the paper, help the children to press out the paper from the fold, smoothing as they go. When dry, cut out for the children, or draw cutting lines around the shape to accentuate a butterfly or moth shape. Wall mount them with the wings slightly open.

Discussion

Discuss the environmental conditions where the butterflies are living – the colour of flowers, the kinds of food and whether it is sunny or shady. Ask the children to predict the colours of the printing, feel the paint underneath the paper, and anticipate where it is going.

Follow-up activities

✧ Use coloured tissue paper, transparent acetate, shiny foil paper, bottle tops and coloured sticky squares to make giant butterflies.
✧ Make symmetrical pictures by pulling loops of string from under thickly painted sugar paper (held down firmly).
✧ Make symmetrical patterns in sticky paper, LEGO, unit counting cubes, and so on.
✧ Make an indoor habitat for caterpillars with a large transparent plastic sweet jar (sometimes available from sweetshops or newsagents). Pierce it for drainage and provide fresh food daily from the place where you collected them.
✧ Explore mirrors, and make and talk about kaleidoscopes and their symmetry.
✧ Sing 'Caterpillar lullaby' in the Scholastic Collections book, *Songs*.

POP-UP PENGUINS

Objective

Design and Technology – To develop skills in making card shapes with movement.

Group size

Four to six children.

What you need

Card (coloured and white), felt-tipped pens or crayons (particularly black), scissors, strong glue or long arm stapler, the activity sheet on page 91 with the penguin, panda and butterfly.

Preparation

Photocopy and cut out card templates of the penguin, panda and butterfly.

Prepare folded pieces of card for the outside of the birthday cards, and for the templates. Make up a sample card following the instructions below.

Instructions:
Cut out the penguins in card and colour in. Fold inwards. Make straight and curved lines to create the beak and tummy (this can be done more easily from the back when folded). Reverse the fold on the beak and legs, and fold the sides of the legs as shown. The penguin is stuck firmly down from head to tail along the inside fold of a separate card and allowed to dry. The panda is done in a similar way; the butterfly card background is coloured from the front, the folds and cuts are made, and the butterfly wings are coloured in when slotted together at the front.

What to do

Ask the children to guess what animal you are, then mime the walk of a penguin by keeping the knees firmly together and elbows stuck to the sides of the body. Reinforce this, or introduce the activity, by asking the children to think of any animals who are – black and white (cats, pandas, horses, etc) – then, black and white and eat fish – finally, black and white and eat fish and live where it is very cold and icy....

Show the children the pop-up penguin card, and ask them to explain how the beak sticks up. Give them the template to help them draw, colour and cut out a penguin (you, or they with help, will need to make the central cuts).

The penguin and panda cards can be decorated on the front and used for a birthday or other event.

Discussion

Black and white are not true colours but the pop-up cards can be used to emphasise the difference between the black and white animals and the coloured butterfly. Discuss the way animals live, how humans can help or destroy their habitats and how the panda is now an endangered species.

Follow-up activities

✧ Let every child make a pop-up black and white penguin or panda card and a coloured butterfly card.

✧ Add the models to a night sights display (see page 61 for ideas).

✧ Read 'Give us back the night' and 'Overnight' in the resources section, page 73.

✧ Ask the children to tell you how they feel about night time – what they find scary at night and what they do to stop feeling scared.

✧ Use an OHP or bright torch to make silhouette pictures of the children's faces on black paper, cut these out and mount them on white.

PATTERN AND MOVEMENT

Objective

PE – To use colour, pattern and sound in movement.

Group size

The whole group.

What you need

Coloured card, crêpe paper, sticky tape, percussion instruments.

Preparation

Cut the crêpe paper into strips. Make coloured card lengths into headbands to fit the children. Arrange space for movement.

What to do

Ask the children to guess which animal you are miming. Make hand movements like a caterpillar, a spider, and a butterfly, then encourage the children to practise themselves. Distribute the headbands and crêpe paper sashes. Now ask the children to move their bodies like animals – for example, those with green headbands and sashes can be caterpillars, with white lambs, black horses, yellow parrots, blue fish, red crabs and so on. Remind them that all animals watch very carefully to avoid bumping into other animals and objects. Encourage suggestions on how long dragons or dinosaurs can be made by forming chains of children wearing different colours in a follow-my-leader animal dance or movement with percussion.

Finish with a 'run and stop' game, based on colours, where the matching children 'freeze'.

Discussion

Ask the children to suggest other coloured animals. This work could be used to prepare for Chinese New Year celebrations when large monsters, lions or dragons dance through the street.

Follow-up activities

✧ Make a lion or dragon head-dress from a painted grocery box with big eye-holes and tissue and foil 'hair'. Attach a colourful body made of old sheeting, spatter-painted or tie-dyed.
✧ Use grocery boxes or other materials to construct a giant dinosaur. Paint this before assembling it upright. (No-one knows what colour dinosaurs were, so the children's suggestions are all valid).
✧ Visit a local zoo, safari park or Natural History Museum to look at animals' skin and hair colour, and movement.
✧ Sing songs and rhymes about animals: 'Going to the zoo' or 'The hippopotamus song' in *Apusskidu* (A & C Black).
✧ Explore ways in which animals balance, or rest in order to sleep.

CHAPTER 3
PLANTS

This chapter looks at colour in the environment and seasonal changes. Children are encouraged to grow plants, as well as consider the conditions needed to support growth. The chapter ends with a traditional celebration of plants and their products at Harvest time.

LEAF COLOURS

Objective

Mathematics – To use leaves and leaf colours as the stimuli for sorting and classification.

Group size

All participating children can be taken on the walk with adult support, activities would work best with four to six children.

What you need

Access to a variety of trees and other plant leaves, scissors or secateurs, thick wax crayons, kitchen or white copy paper, a skewer or pointed tool, card, hoops or Venn rings, paint and brushes, sponges.

Preparation

Plan a route for a collecting walk with easy and safe access to leaves that vary noticeably in size, shape and colour. The walk can take place in summer or autumn – the different greens will vary enough to comment upon, although autumn colours are more stimulating. Tree or bush leaves are usually stronger than ground plants and can stand up to the wear and tear of rubbings and painting.

Identify, draw and cut out some coloured card leaf shapes and score deep veins on them using a pointed tool. Write the leaf name on the other side.

What to do

Take the children on the walk, asking them to act as detectives to find and collect samples of different leaves. Once back in your room, ask the children to sort the leaves. Encourage them to use their own criteria, as well as colour, shape, and so on.

Use the prepared card shapes for comparison and try to identify the leaves (using information books, if necessary).

Make leaf rubbings and leaf prints. Use the underside of the original leaves or scored card shapes, with either white paper and wax crayons or colour paint put on by sponges or brushes.

Discussion

Remind the children not to take too many leaves as these collect sunlight and provide the tree with food. Ask the children 'Which leaves belong together?' (for example sorting yellow/green, prickly/not prickly, shiny/dull).

Follow-up activities

✧ Use the prints and rubbings to make pictures – try a tree with a bark-rubbing trunk and leaf-printed canopy or a butterfly from two leaf prints; even a magic carpet or a sari made with prints and rubbings from many leaves.

✧ Use the leaves and prints for counting. Do all the horse-chestnut leaves have the same number of 'fingers'? What about our hands? Encourage counting in 5s.

✧ Say the action poem 'The autumn leaves' in the resources section on page 69.

LOOKING FOR COLOUR

Objective

Art – To encourage the children to observe and record colour and shapes from direct experience.

Group size

Introduce to the whole group, but paint in smaller groups of four to six children.

What you need

Various art materials for drawing, colouring and painting – wax crayons, pastels, paints, brushes, and so on, a bunch of flowers (fresh or everlasting), fruit or vegetables in a bowl.

Preparation

Make up a bowl of fruit or vegetables. Try to include one or two less familiar ones such as mango and sweet potato. Fill a vase with flowers. Find a safe place for these on or near the painting area.

What to do

Let the children look at, and if possible handle, the flowers or fruit, and discuss colours, shape, shiny surface and texture. Encourage their descriptions after feeling, smelling and looking underneath. Return the objects to the bowl or vase and reinforce their observations with a 'mime' guessing game. Begin the game by miming a fruit or flower, showing the shape with hands or fingers, or simply 'drawing' it in the air. When guessed correctly, hold up the object and trace its outline again with a finger. Give the children the opportunity to draw and paint pictures of the fruit and flowers.

Discussion

Ask the children if all the flowers or fruit are different and if anything is the same. Encourage them to describe the petals, colour of skin, pattern, and so on. Make your own exploratory observational drawings alongside and involve the children in your decisions – 'I wonder if this colour will....' 'Maybe if I try this one instead, it will....'; 'What colour do you think it is, Jason?'.

Follow-up activities

✧ Encourage the children's awareness of contrasting colours by allowing them to choose the colour for mounting their paintings.

✧ Use other plants for the same exercise – try cacti (with care), savoy cabbage, different fruits, leeks or onions.

✧ Visit a local art gallery and look for 'still life' pictures.

✧ Display the children's framed pictures as a gallery exhibition, then invite parents and friends. The children could design invitations for this.

✧ Make cards for St. Valentine's Day, Mothers' Day, or Easter with tissue paper flowers or acrylic observational drawings done directly on to the front of the cards.

✧ Look at and grow some seeds in pots and write a growth diary.

✧ Sing and dance 'In and out the dusty bluebells'.

✧ Read and discuss 'The dormouse and the doctor' in *When We Were Very Young* by A. A. Milne (Methuen), in which the sleepy dormouse, who loves 'delphiniums blue and geraniums red', is prescribed 'chrysanthemums yellow and white', which simply makes him more determined than ever to keep his eyes shut tight!

✧ Read the action poem 'My window-box' on page 68 of the resources section.

CHANGING COLOUR

❋ ❋

Objective

Science — To observe the changes that occur when coloured liquids are added to water, exploring floating and sinking (density), and mixing.

Group size

Four to six children.

What you need

Clear transparent containers, as narrow as possible (measuring cylinders, jars, plastic soda or tonic bottles), clear plastic cups for drinking, vegetable oil, detergent, bright food colourings, coloured squashes, (blackcurrant, orange, lime), small spoons, eye-droppers, salt, small jugs.

Preparation

If you are using plastic bottles as containers, cut off the tops evenly to make investigations easier. Give each group three containers with a little oil in one and the other two three-quarters full of fresh water and very salty water respectively. Make sure the drinking cups are clean.

What to do

Show the children the containers with water, salty water and oil. Ask them for predictions of what will happen when drops of food colouring are added to each one. Let the children add drops from small spoons or eye-droppers, without stirring, observing the behaviour of the colouring through the side. Encourage them to explain the differences. Try stirring, pausing, then adding a few drops of detergent, and stirring again.

Give the children the clean cups three-quarters filled with fresh water and ask them to predict the effect of adding one of the coloured squashes, then another. Let them add spoonfuls of squash, without stirring, then stirring and tasting.

Discussion

Ask the children why they think the colouring behaves as it does. Food colourings have different densities relative to the two forms of water and oil. Young children are likely to say 'it's heavier', 'it's not strong enough', or 'it just floats', all of which are acceptable *early* concepts. Discuss which liquid *they* would float best in — remind them that the sea is salty!

Follow-up activities

✧ If there is access to a freezer, use some coloured squash mixtures to make ice lollies and slush drinks (ice-cubes of squash broken up in a blender).
✧ Put a little food colouring into the water tray to extend play with tubing and plastic bottles.
✧ Make milk shakes with bananas, raspberries, blackberries (fresh or frozen) or coloured milk shake flavourings.
✧ Make a display of coloured liquids in different sized and shaped containers on a window-sill set against the light.
✧ In movement lessons, ask the children to move like the food colourings dropped into the bottles and in two groups show how the salty water 'pushes away' the other liquids.
✧ Sing the song 'Colour splash' on page 83 of the resources section.

PLANTS AND COLOUR

Objective

Science — To investigate growth and colour in plants.

Group size

Four to six children.

What you need

Blotting paper or felt cloth, black sugar paper, carnations or celery, food colourings, jars, saucers or lids, white cloth or paper, various seeds, such as sunflower, grass, dried peas, runner beans, peanuts, a coconut, cloves, sesame seeds, red kidney beans (vary the size, colour, shape), any seasonal flowers, hand lenses.

Preparation

Prepare for the experiments you have selected (see suggestions below).

What to do

Put groups of different seeds on to white cloth or paper in the centre of the group and discuss the different colours, first without touching, then after looking at them closely with hand lenses.

Show any seasonal flowers and look at the seeds in their seed pods. Then investigate plant colour by carrying out one, or more, of these experiments:
✧ Grow cress seeds on two pieces of blotting paper or felt cloth. Keep both watered, but cover one in black paper.
✧ Stand celery pieces or white carnations in one container of plain water and another which holds water mixed with bright red or blue food colouring.
✧ Put a thick collar of damp blotting paper inside large jam jars. Insert red kidney beans or dried green peas between the blotting paper and the sides of the jar. Water carefully each day, making sure excess water drains away and watch the roots and seedlings grow, noting any colour changes.

Discussion

Ask the children to find as many similarities as possible (especially comparing a coconut with the tiny seeds inside a clove head) then explain they are all seeds. Encourage the children to suggest what type of plant might grow from each seed, the colour, and the size of the plants.

Be sure to emphasise safety when handling seeds and remind children not to eat the seeds and to wash their hands before eating.

Follow-up activities

✧ Use the following list to grow plants indoors or outside to coincide with the children's birthday months. Display with the children's names.
January: snowdrops, hyacinths, amaryllis, honesty (silver seed heads);
February: snowdrops, crocuses, dwarf irises;
March: anemones, daffodils, primulas;
April: narcissi, polyanthus, honesty (flowers);
May: tulips, busy Lizzies, pansies;
June: antirrhinum, stock, sweet peas;
July: petunias, perennial dahlias, begonias;
August: delphiniums, geraniums;
September: sunflowers, sweet peas, zinnias;
October: begonias, godetia, Michaelmas daisies;
November: cyclamen, autumn crocus, chinese lanterns;
December: aconites, winter jasmine, cotoneaster. (Some flowers could be used with different colours for several months, for example busy Lizzies.)
✧ Use the different seeds to create collage pictures and patterns.
✧ Buy some wild bird seed (from pet shops) and use the mixture first for sorting, then for feeding birds through the winter.

GARDENER'S WORLD

Objective

English – To develop skills in organising writing for information purposes.

Group size

Introduce to all, but work with groups of four to six children for the writing activity.

What you need

Packet of wild bird seed, other coloured seeds and pulses, A4 paper, sticky tape or glue sticks, pencils, apple, orange (not seedless), strawberries or blackberries, passion fruit, fig or tamarillo (or any other coloured fruit with lots of seeds), avocado or mango (or anything else with one large seed), cutting board and knife.

Preparation

Prepare an appropriate vocabulary sheet, for example: apple, orange, blackberry, seed, grow, water, drink, soil, sun, put, pot. Make a sign for the home corner which says 'Garden Shop'. Make up a simple, open seed packet by folding an A4 sheet into three, and sticking down the sides and base (as shown below).

What to do

Look at the fruit and ask the children to describe the colours in the skins, and predict the colours inside the fruit – flesh and seeds – then cut and see. Pour out some of the wild bird seed and discuss the colours and possible growth. (Remind children that many seeds are not safe to eat.)

Put some of the seeds into the empty paper seed packet and discuss the kind of information needed on the packet to help people grow the seeds (for example, name, planting instructions and so on).

Make packets with simple instructions, such as 'Put the peas in some soil. Give them a drink of water' or simply label them, for example 'Sunflowers'. Draw pictures on the back of the packet, to show how the seeds will look when they grow, and the price, for example '5p'. Put different seeds into the packets, seal them, then set up a display for sale in the Garden Shop.

Discussion

Encourage the children to offer alternative thoughts and ideas by asking questions such as 'Anything else?' and 'Will black and white seeds grow into black and white plants? Brown seeds into brown plants?' to invite speculative responses and hypotheses. Do they know where seeds grow on a plant?

Follow-up activities

✧ Taste test with the remaining fruit.
✧ Grow some of the seeds, particularly those which are easy to grow, such as runner beans, cress, sunflowers, nasturtium.
✧ Make up pot plants with tissue paper flowers on sticks stuck into plastic pots filled with modelling clay, price them, and 'sell' them in the shop.
✧ Bring in dried grasses or dried flowers to add colour, texture and reality to the shop.
✧ Make up adding cards with flowers and fruit and prices '2p' and '3p' to use with toy money.
✧ Read and dramatise 'Jack and the Beanstalk' (Ladybird or another version).
✧ Sing 'Colour splash', on page 83.

AUTUMN LEAVES

Objective

Music – To enjoy and represent events in the environment in sound.

Group size

Whole group.

What you need

Enough musical instruments for each child to have one, variously coloured autumn leaves, dry dead leaves, cassette recorder and tape (if possible).

Preparation

If possible, record some sounds such as walking through dry leaves, the wind in the trees, the sound of rain, and so on.

What to do

Ask the children to look at the colours of the leaves, then close their eyes and listen to the sounds you make by rustling fresh leaves together or crumpling dry leaves. (Play the taped sounds at this point.) Ask the children to echo the sounds with musical instruments. Remind them of the original sounds periodically between playing.

When they have got the idea of this, ask them to accompany the following story, playing at the end of each sentence, listening for quiet places and loud ones.

Once upon a time in the spring the sun began to shine and the horse chestnut tree began to open its sticky buds...
The leaves spread out their fingers, growing bigger and bigger and bigger...
The rain came...
... And once a big thunderstorm with thunder and lightning...
Then the sun came out again...
The weather got colder and the wind began to blow...
Conkers fell off the tree, plop, plop, plop...
The leaves turned yellow, gold, red and brown and they rustled as they fell to the ground...
At last the tree was bare and the quiet snow began to fall...
The tree slept and waited for spring. (end)

Discuss their choice of sounds. Change instruments and play again.

Discussion

Ask the children to listen to the differences between the fresh, coloured autumn leaves and the dry brown ones. Ask them to focus on 'rustling' sounds, then bang the tambourine or shaker very loudly. If the children protest, ask if they can show *you* how to make the right sounds.

Follow-up activities

✧ Do more actions with the poem 'The autumn leaves' on page 69.
✧ Restrict painting colours to two shades of red, two of yellow, two of brown and two of green. Mount and display the results as 'Autumn Colours'.
✧ Cut templates of different leaves to draw around and colour in. Hang the paper leaves as a mobile from a coat hanger, or use them to make an 'Autumn Trees' collage with twigs.

RATTLE AND SHAKE

Objective

Design and Technology – To design and make tall colourful plants with seed heads.

Group size

Five or six children at a time.

What you need

A few colourful seasonal flowers with long stems and, if possible, seed heads (daffodils, honesty, buttercups, dandelions, sunflowers or chrysanthemums), plentiful supplies of craft materials including kitchen roll tubes or poster tubes, florists' sticks or dry twigs, adhesive, sticky tape, paints, coloured tissue paper or crêpe paper, newspaper, margarine tubs with lids, different kinds of seeds and pulses (sunflower seeds, dried peas, grass seed, broad beans and so on), coloured sticky labels.

Preparation

Make 'mystery' boxes with the seeds and pulses in different margarine tubs, identified by coloured labels – have one with a dandelion clock if possible. Lay out paints and materials to match the flowers or seed heads brought in, for example brown buttons, yellow paint, or black tissue paper.

What to do

Shake the mystery boxes one at a time. Ask the children to predict what is inside – its colour, size, feel, and so on. Open each box and discuss the contents – the type of plant, colours, and so on. Show the flower samples and discuss the colours and shapes of the stems, petals and centres. Talk about ways of making tall plants with seed 'heads' or seed 'boxes' at the top inside the flower.

Working individually, or in groups, let the children use any of the materials to build tall flowers with coloured petals, to stand on the table

top or a giant one standing on the floor. Use the seeds from the mystery boxes stuck directly on to the flower head or in sealed boxes (small fromage frais pots work well). Show how a little shake or some gentle blowing might rattle or dislodge the seeds from the flower.

Discussion

Can the children guess why the seeds are usually in the flower head at the top of a tall stem? Can they think of different ways that seeds can travel to new places to grow?

Show how precarious a poster tube or rolled up newspaper is when standing upright. Can the children think of ways to make it stable, besides sticking it to the floor?

Follow-up activities

✧ Display the tall flower models in a group on a green cloth or paper background.
✧ Measure the height of the flowers and put them in order, or represent them with sticky paper strips on a bar chart.
✧ Read 'My window-box' on page 68.
✧ Read 'The dormouse and the doctor' in *When We Were Very Young* by A. A. Milne (Methuen).
✧ Use seeds to make colourful musical shakers.

HARVEST FESTIVAL

Objective

PE – To increase confidence and skills in body control, particularly when stretching and rolling.

Group size

The whole group.

What you need

Various fruits and vegetables, for example apple and banana, potato and carrot, pomegranate and cucumber (select these from an existing Harvest display of gifts or use this activity to encourage contributions), space to move, PE mats, low apparatus.

Preparation

None.

What to do

Show the fruit and vegetables, then mime one of these with your hands or whole body, asking the children to guess which fruit you are. Let the children show their body shapes as apples, bananas, potatoes and carrots. Play a running or skipping game giving commands such as 'Apple' (crouch down in a rolled shape), or 'Banana' (stretch or jump high).

Work on mats and low apparatus going across or along them in these two shapes, tucking tightly up or stretching out. Older children can reinforce techniques of jumping (tall) off apparatus and rolling up on landing. Ask the children to suggest movements to represent kiwi-fruit (hairy), or pineapples (with prickles), squashy blackberries, cherry 'twins' and enormous pumpkins, and finish off with everyone joining together as 'a bunch of grapes'.

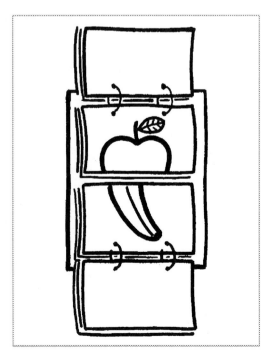

Discussion

Ask 'How many parts of you can you roll up small?', 'Can you make yourself the longest carrot / banana in the room?' Some young children cannot manage a forward roll. Ask 'How many different ways can you roll – forwards? sideways?'

Follow-up activities

✧ Ask the children to predict the inside colour of the fruit and vegetables, then cut them open – the long ones cut lengthwise to emphasise this characteristic (as shown below). Whenever possible

include foods from around the world. Eat some and use others for painting shapes – try potato, apple, carrot and cucumber.

✧ Use modelling clay to make models of the fruits and vegetables, baking where appropriate. Encourage the children to match the colour and shape of the originals.

✧ Sing 'Harvest' in the Scholastic Collections book, *Songs* and 'Harvest' in *Sing a Song One* (Nelson).

✧ Make a matching food flip book. Draw bold outlines of about ten fruits and vegetables on to card and punch holes in the tops. Cut the food cards in half and punch holes in their bases. Cut a strong base card slightly bigger than the food cards and punch holes at the top and base. Fasten the cards to this with string or food bag ties so that they flip over (see illustration). Children can then colour them, match and discuss.

✧ Write Harvest poems and mount them on silhouette shapes of fruit and vegetables, as shown.

✧ Make fruit salad or vegetable soup.

CHAPTER 4
FOOD

Colour has a big influence on how we view food and this chapter explores our attitudes and tastes. The activities are set in international contexts — geographical, cultural and religious — and show that food, and the shared preparation and eating of it, is truly a cause for celebration.

PASTA PATTERNS

Objective

Art — To explore the use of pattern and texture.

Group size

Introduce to all, then work with groups of four to six children.

What you need

Varieties of shaped pasta, such as spaghetti, tagliatelle, macaroni, butterfly and twisted; food colourings (red, green, yellow and blue), glue and glue spreaders, thick card, jugs or bowls and spoons.

Preparation

Cut the card into circles and squares approximately 15-18 cm across. Dye some pasta shapes by dipping them quickly into water containing several drops of bright colouring (250ml colouring solution will dye approximately 250 grams of pasta). Allow these to dry on kitchen paper.

What to do

Ask a child to stand. Say a colour and let the other children name all the items of clothing of that colour the child is wearing. Repeat this with other children and other colours.

Change the game to patterns... such as 'dots', 'stripes', 'zigzags', 'flowers', 'all one colour'. Discuss how we can recognise 'a pattern' and which patterns they like to wear. Ask them to describe patterns on the carpet, floor, walls, furniture or displays. Show the square and circular cards and encourage suggestions as to how patterns could be made on these shapes.

Then ask the children to choose a card shape and make a pattern by sticking on the pasta.

Ask them to decide whether they will begin from the edge or the centre of the circle, work in rows or round the edges of the square. Allow the patterns to dry, then display them on a table or varnish and pin them on a wall.

Discussion

Young children sometimes 'lose track' of their original pattern, or get diverted by another one. Praise existing patterns and ask 'What colour came before this one?' or 'What colour/shape will you use next?'

Follow-up activities

✧ Cook some shapes from the left-over untreated pasta in boiling water as directed on the packet. Serve with tomato ketchup and/or grated cheese.
✧ Let the children practise tongue twisters, saying them faster and faster, for example:
'I like pizza, I like pasta';
'Patsy likes pizza but Peter likes pasta'.
✧ Use a number board with coloured unit cubes to make coloured number patterns — such as every third one red or every fifth one yellow, and so on.
✧ Go for a pattern walk to buildings or shops, encouraging the children to look at colours and patterns in walls or in shop windows.

FESTIVAL SWEETS

Objective

RE – To encourage awareness of how cultures and faiths celebrate by sharing foods.

Group size

Introduce to the whole group but cook with groups of four to six children.

What you need

A large, clean table, ingredients for sweets (see below), sweet cases, coloured tissue paper circles, narrow coloured ribbons, large spoons, bowls, empty chocolate boxes, Easter egg cases, modelling clay.

Preparation

Cut ribbons into lengths for tying.

What to do

Show the empty chocolate box and Easter egg case and discuss special occasions when sweets are given as gifts (birthdays, Christmas, Eid, Easter).

Describe other celebrations such as Chinese New Year when people give each other sweets, especially children, or Iranian weddings when special sweets are made for the families and friends to enjoy together.

Make festival sweets by taking 500g icing sugar, four or five tablespoons of full-cream condensed milk, food colourings and flavourings, nuts (check for allergies with parents), coconut and cherries (halve the ingredients if you have two groups). Sift the icing sugar into a bowl and blend in the condensed milk until the mixture is smooth and creamy (this may take a little time). Divide the paste into two or three and add one or two drops of a flavouring or colouring to each. Add a little water if the mixture remains very dry. Roll into small balls and coat in coconut or icing sugar and add an almond, a walnut piece or half a glacé cherry.

Press into the sweet cases and leave to set (these quantities should make about 90 sweets).

Choose a selection and put into large circles of tissue paper and tie with ribbon (red only for Chinese New Year, but use different colours with matching ribbons for an Iranian 'wedding').

Discussion

Discuss the reasons and the feelings people have for giving special sweets, and the effect on the persons receiving them.

Many children receive sweets frequently – this shows family affection but needs careful monitoring. Ask the children how they care for their teeth and how often they visit the dentist.

If they had some special sweets who would they like to give them to, and why?

Follow-up activities

✧ Celebrate Chinese New Year in the home corner by having a big spring clean.
✧ Read about Alfie being a page boy in *The Big Alfie and Annie Rose Storybook* by Shirley Hughes (Red Fox) and use clothes from the role-play box for marriage ceremonies.
✧ Read about Jesus at the marriage feast when he turned water into wine for the celebrations (in *The Ladybird Bible Story Book*, or *Piccolo Child's Bible*).
✧ Use modelling clay to make 'chocolates' for chocolate boxes, or Easter eggs. Decorate the home corner and have a 'pretend' celebration.
✧ Sing 'Can you taste the colour?' on page 82 of the resources section.

THEMES
for early years

RECIPES FROM AROUND THE WORLD

Objective
Geography – To develop the children's awareness of places other than their own locality.

Group size
Eight to twelve children.

What you need
Choose from the following foods (bearing in mind the origins of any children in the group): poppadoms, slices from a round loaf topped with tomato purée and cheddar cheese (mini-pizzas), prawn crackers, Turkish delight, halva; frying pan, cooking utensils, coloured card, writing and colouring tools.

Preparation
Cut the coloured cards into squares or oblongs approximately ¼ A4 size with three or four pieces of each colour.

Use the list below, or your own, to write out the country of origin, name of food and greetings on coloured cards.

Pizza	Italy	Buon giorno
Poppadoms	India	Namaste
Halva	Greece	Kalymera
Cheddar cheese	England	Good morning

What to do
Show the children a few of the 'international' foods such as prawn crackers or turkish delight. Invite the children to guess the country of origin.

Shuffle and give out the cards to the children and ask them to sort themselves into groups by the colour on their card.

Then read out the words on the cards with each colour group, encouraging the children to join in. Reshuffle and deal out the cards again a few times, with the children sorting themselves into different colour groups each time and rehearsing the country, greeting and food.

Choose one or two colour groups to make or prepare a food while the other children decorate their cards with felt-tipped pens or crayons on the back and around the border of the reading side.

Mini-pizzas: Lightly toast slices of a round loaf, spread a thin layer of tomato purée on top followed by grated cheddar cheese. Grill until the cheese bubbles, cool and eat.

Poppadoms: Follow the instructions or cook quickly in enough hot vegetable oil to cover one at a time, drain on kitchen paper and eat.

Serve Chinese prawn crackers, Turkish delight and Greek halva on saucers or plates.

Discussion
Ask children to describe the different foods they have tasted here and in other countries. Make sure the children know of the great range of foods available in each country.

Follow-up activities
✧ Ask the children to predict the changes to the food – the colours, the 'cooking' sounds, the smells, flavours and tastes.
✧ Add cards to each set showing that country's flag, coloured in by the children.

FRUIT AND NUT KHOSHAF

Objective

RE – To encourage children to value their own and other food rituals in world religions.

Group size

Five to six children at a time.

What you need

250g dried apricots, 250g dried dates, 250g prunes, 150g seedless raisins, 100g pine nuts*, 100g sliced almonds*, 150g sultanas, 100g walnut pieces*, a little honey or syrup, small dishes, bowls, spoons, small knives, a few fresh grapes (green and black), apricots and plums (if in season). (*Check for allergies)

Preparation

Divide up the ingredients equally, according to the number of groups of children. Put the ingredients into separate dishes.

What to do

Ask the children to tell you what they had for breakfast – the colour and taste. Ask them to describe the different fruits and nuts, first *without*, then *with* touching, the colours, textures and shapes. Show them the fresh fruit and compare with the dried fruits.

Explain that Muslims fast between dawn and sunset during Ramadan to celebrate the sending of their Holy Book, the Qur'an, and to remind them of the many hungry people around the world. After the sun has set, they eat simple sustaining foods, such as Khoshaf.

Point out that Christians also fast during Lent to remind them of the time when Jesus went without food. Buddhists and Hindus fast too, and Jewish people at Yom Kippur.

Let the children taste each food, describing texture and flavour. Chop up the walnuts into smaller pieces, and cut up the dried apricots, dates and prunes. Put the fruits into a bowl, cover with water and leave overnight. The following day, drain, and discuss any changes in colour and shape.

Add the nuts. Thin some honey with water and pour tablespoonfuls of this over the mixture to coat the fruit and nuts.

Serve small portions in bowls and let the children eat with spoons.

Discussion

Some children will have eaten fruit and nuts fresh, or in cereal mixtures. Ask the children what it feels like when they're really hungry. What would it be like if they had no food for days and days? Can they suggest ways to help children who don't have enough to eat?

Follow-up activities

✧ Make pancakes, celebrated in many faiths. When cooked, add honey or syrup (roll up for Shrove Tuesday or Mardi Gras pancakes) and possibly chopped nuts (folded in half for Ramadan Kataif).
✧ Make up poems about the different fruits and nuts using colour and texture vocabulary, for example:
    Golden apricots
    Soft brown dates
    Hard yellow pine nuts
    Wrinkled black prunes.....
✧ Dress up in colourful costumes for a Mardi Gras Carnival and dance to music.
✧ Weigh some of the dried fruits before and after soaking overnight. Record and discuss the results.
✧ Learn the poem by Christina Rossetti:
    Mix a pancake
    Stir a pancake
    Pop it in the pan
    Fry the pancake
    Toss the pancake
    Catch it if you can.

TEN GREEN BOTTLES

Objective

PE – To play some games that involve simple rules and equipment.

Group size

All participating children.

What you need

Large plastic mineral water bottles (approximately the same number as children in the group) or similar with rounded bases (green if possible), some sort of weighting material, such as modelling clay, small beads or marbles, or beans and seeds; beanbags, small bags.

Preparation

Turn the bottles into 'skittles' by weighting them inside to give them a little stability – enough to remain upright when set up by young children with limited motor skills, but still fairly easy to knock down with beanbags or light balls. Use available 'weighting' material such as beans, marbles or modelling clay to stabilise the bottles – close the lids tightly.

What to do

Teach the children the countdown song about ten green bottles:

Ten green bottles standing on the wall
(repeat)
... And if one green bottle should accidentally fall,
There'd be nine green bottles standing on the wall.
Nine green bottles... *(and so on)*...

Take turns to play a game with ten children standing upright on a mat or low bench as the bottles while the other children dance around them, clapping on the word 'fall' as one by one the 'bottles' crouch down or jump down.

Divide the children into smaller groups to practise aiming and throwing. Each group of three or four children will need three or four skittles standing fairly close together, within fairly easy range, and beanbags or balls for throwing. Encourage 'group' success as well as individual achievement.

Discussion

Ask what might happen if green *glass* bottles fell down, and why we all need to jump down carefully and land softly.

Follow-up activities

✧ Emphasise 'jumping down in safety' as a focus for movements by playing the game on low and higher apparatus.
✧ Make a number frieze, with the children drawing, cutting out (from a template) and painting ten green bottles with numerals on the front.

✧ Read the title poem in *Now We are Six* by A.A. Milne ('When I was one, I had just begun...').
✧ Sing 'The animals went in two by two' and 'Ten in a bed' in *Apusskidu* (A & C Black).
✧ Do the action rhyme 'Colour counting', on page 67 of the resources section.

ALL SORTS OF SWEETS

Objective

Mathematics – To develop colour recognition while sorting.

Group size

Introduce to the whole group, but do the wrapping and sorting with four to six children.

What you need

Transparent plastic jars of different sizes with wide necks and screw-top lids (ask local shops for plastic sweet containers, which are often thrown away when empty), modelling clay (a few strong colours and white), Cellophane sweet wrappers or coloured tissue paper.

Preparation

Make up some sweet shapes from the modelling clay. Wrap roughly equal numbers in each colour, then mix them together in one of the containers.

What to do

Show the children the jar full of wrapped coloured sweets. Explain that the colours have got mixed up and ask them to help you sort them out into empty containers. Say the colours aloud as you sort, testing their observation with a deliberate mistake now and then. Discuss which colour has wrapped the most sweets. Count them out together.

Let the children make some small modelling clay or play dough sweets. These can then be sorted into jars and put into the home corner or used for a sweet shop or a newsagent's with sweets, newspapers and magazines for sale.

Discussion

Ask the children to estimate which jar of sweets has the most, the fewest, and what they would do to check this.

Ask them to guess how many sweets each jar might hold, and if it would make a difference if they used big sweets or little ones. Throughout, emphasise that no-one should try to eat the 'pretend' sweets.

Follow-up activities

✧ Play the sorting and counting game on other occasions, remembering to vary the number of sweets but keeping the numbers low so that children can count with confidence.
✧ Make coloured lollipops from lolly sticks with modelling clay or card circles stuck on (see page 93). Display these in a small pot, weighted inside for stability.
✧ Look at the effect of the coloured Cellophane – can the children guess the colour of the modelling clay before unwrapping?
✧ Discuss the effect of eating sweets on teeth and the importance of regular teeth-cleaning and visits to the dentist. Can they think of foods they like that are good for teeth?
✧ Make some games for a school fête, Open Day or fund-raising event, for example, estimating the total number of each colour of wooden beads or sweets in the jars or the weight of the cakes made with clay or dough, then coloured and baked.
✧ Sing 'Can you taste the colour?' on page 82.

CAN YOU TASTE THE COLOUR?

Objective

Science – To investigate the connection between colour and flavour.

Group size

Four to six children.

What you need

Food colourings, two or three packets of instant mashed potato powder, bowls, spoons, kettle, jug, sharp knife, red apples, green apples, three or four packets of crisps with different flavours and colours, (for example prawn, smoky bacon, plain, chicken), hand lenses, plates or saucers, colourful pictures of fruit.

Preparation

Check on children's allergies or cultural restrictions with any of the above foods. Ask the children to wash their hands.

What to do

Show the children the crisps in their different coloured packets and discuss why the manufacturers have used different colours. Tip the crisps into saucers and discuss the colour of the crisps. Look at them closely with hand lenses. Do a 'blind' taste test with one child at a time. Eyes should be kept closed until the flavour of the crisp has been guessed.

Make up the instant mashed potato with the children, following the instructions on the packet, but adding drops of different food colouring to the measured hot water to make red, green or blue mashed potato. Give each child small quantities of each colour and a spoon. Do 'blind' taste-testing again – encouraging the children to describe taste, texture, smell (if any) and colour. Finish by taste-testing the pieces of red and green apple.

Discussion

The children may wish to assert that they *can* taste colour (food colourings do vary) so accept all responses. Tell them that in factories some foods are deliberately coloured, such as sweets, frozen peas, jams and jellies. Ask the children to suggest reasons for colouring food (flavour, attraction, identification) or not. Explain that sometimes people can have an allergic reaction to the extra colourings or 'additives' in foods.

Follow-up activities

◇ Use the mashed potato (coloured or uncoloured) to make any of the following:

Yorkshire potato cakes: Add an equal amount of self-raising flour to the potato and a pinch of salt. Mould into a dough using a little water if necessary, and roll out on a floured board. Cut into squares and bake in a moderate oven (180°C, Gas Mark 4). Cool, butter (or substitute) and eat.

Latkes: Add an equal volume of grated onion, a pinch of salt and mould into thick flat pancakes. Fry gently on both sides in a little vegetable oil, cool and eat.

Cheesy potato scones: Add equal volumes of grated cheddar cheese and a pinch of salt, mould into thick flat scones and grill lightly on both sides. Cool, butter (or substitute) and eat.

◇ Sing 'I know they're bad for my teeth' and 'My friend Billy loves bubble gum' in the Scholastic Collections book, *Songs*.

◇ Sing 'Can you taste the colour?' on page 82.

JELLIES FOR A PARTY

Objective
Science – To develop knowledge and understanding of dissolving.

Group size
Four to six children at a time.

What you need
Sea salt (large crystals), white sugar cubes, coloured jellies (perhaps red, green, orange and black), trifle cases, transparent cups or clean jam jars, transparent mixing bowls, spoons, kettle, paper towels, drinking water, pieces of seasonal fruit (apple, banana, strawberries, oranges).

Advance preparation
Create space in a refrigerator for setting several jellies. Ask the children to wash their hands.

What to do
Let the child explore the salt crystals by looking at them and tasting one, then adding them to their own half-cupful of warm drinking water. Ask the children to stir and watch the crystals 'disappear', then suggest where the salt has gone. Encourage the children to taste the salty water with a finger.

Repeat the exercise with cubes of sugar. The children should now be able to explain how the sweetness of the sugar is still there. Encourage them to use the word 'dissolved', as well as 'disappeared' or 'gone into the water'.

Next, use cubes of coloured jelly in mixing bowls, dividing the cubes and a little hot water equally between the children. Make it up to the required amount with cold water.

Let the children choose pieces of fruit to match or contrast with the coloured jelly. Put them into the trifle cases, then pour over the liquid jelly. Leave them to set in the fridge.

If possible, invite children from another group to share the jellies at a 'party' or link this with the activity 'Party hats and invitations' on page 45.

Discussion
'Dissolving' is a difficult concept and is often confused with 'melting' where a solid object becomes liquid when warmed or heated. Dissolving jelly cubes will need adult assistance.

Follow-up activities
✧ Vary the jelly mixtures by using sparkling mineral water or lemonade to top up the jelly cubes (dissolved in hot water).
✧ Make a very strong salt solution by dissolving as much as possible in a cupful of water (a supersaturated solution). Fasten a piece of knotted string on a pencil and suspend it over the salt solution so that the knotted string is in the liquid (see below). Leave this in a warm place and watch the salt crystals 'reappear' as the water evaporates over a few days.

✧ Let the children move like jellies to the following rhyme:

Red jelly on a plate,
Wibble, wibble, wobble,
Wibble, wibble, wobble,
Red jelly on a plate,
Jelly then goes splat!
(Children sink to the floor.)

Change the colour of the jelly and repeat the game.

CHAPTER 5
OUT AND ABOUT

This chapter explores different places and events in our lives and colours in the world around us. Some provide stability, like our homes and annual festivals, while others are less predictable – a circus clown, or an unexpected invitation.

BUSES AND MOTOR CARS

Objective

Music – To use vehicle colours as a stimulus for singing.

Group size

Groups of four to six children at a time for colouring and cutting, though the whole group can join in the singing.

What you need

The song 'Motor car' in Scholastic Collections, *Songs,* the song 'The wheels on the bus', and templates cut from the activity sheets on pages 92 and 93 respectively, paints or crayons, a hole punch and split pins.

Preparation

Prepare a car and a bus with wheels using the templates on the activity sheets. Colour one side but leave the windows empty.

What to do

Show the children the vehicles and discuss the ways they travel to school, the shops, or to visit relatives. Ask them to describe the colour of their local bus, or family car if they have one. Sing or say 'The wheels on the bus', with actions. Introduce the motor car song.

Let the children choose and colour one of the vehicles, then cut these out. Cut out two wheels for each vehicle, punch holes where needed and fasten the split pins in place. Sing the songs again with the children making their vehicle wheels 'go round' while they sing about the bus.

In the motor car song, add verses such as... 'Red car, red car...' and 'Green bus, green bus...' so that the children can identify their own vehicles with the words of the song.

Discussion

Ask the children who is driving the car or the bus and who the passengers might be. If they could choose the colour of the bus or car they usually travel in, what would they like it to be? Can they recognise the right bus by its colour? What colours do lollipop men and women at road crossings wear so we can recognise them?

Follow-up activities

✧ With adult support, go for a walk and look at the colours of the staff cars, or the parked cars in a nearby street or passing by. Make a chart of the colours seen.
✧ Ask the children to bring in toy vehicles for sorting activities.
✧ Read *The Big Red Bus Ride* by Peter Curry (Collins) for sequencing and reading maps.
✧ Make an enlarged photocopy of the map on page 88 and use it with small toy cars.
✧ Invite a police officer or lollipop person to your group to discuss road safety.

MY DOOR COLOUR

Objective

Geography – To increase awareness of human features in the children's local area.

Group size

The whole group can go on the walk, but break into groups of four to six children for the activity.

What you need

Camera, card, A4 size drawing paper, writing and colouring tools such as pencils, crayons or pastels, adhesive, sticky tape, scissors.

Preparation

Arrange extra adult help, then plan a walk that passes by some of the children's homes. This should take no longer than half an hour.

Cut card into A4 sizes, one card for each child plus one spare. Mark each card with a door and two windows. Complete one to represent *your* home, cutting the sides of the door and windows so that they open. Colour your door and number it. Position a piece of A4 drawing paper behind it, stick it in place, then draw yourself and other people behind the door and windows (see below).

What to do

Show the children your home door card and encourage them to describe the door colour, the shape or pattern, and the number on the door. Open the 'door' to show the picture of yourself, and others in the windows.

Ask the children to recall and describe their own door colour, pattern, and number.

Take the children on the walk, stopping to look at doors that you pass, especially their own. Encourage them to describe the colour, any shapes they can see in the door, the position of the letter-box, number and keyhole, which side the hinge is on and the materials used to make the door. Take photographs of these and other local doors, think about including a shop, a church or a fire station.

Back at base, ask the children to colour and add patterns to their card homes, then cut the door and windows to open as above. Glue the card on to the A4 drawing paper, avoiding the openings. Let the children make drawings of themselves and their families in the open windows and doors. Children with few family members may wish to draw a pet, a friend or a cuddly toy.

Discussion

Ask 'What is behind the door?', 'Who is beside you?' (or below, above, in front of), 'What is the colour of the back door, or your bedroom door?' and so on.

Follow-up activities

✧ Display the children's doors in numerical order, and make a chart of door colours (see below).

What colour is your door?				
red	brown	green	blue	white
🚪				
🚪		🚪	🚪	
🚪	🚪	🚪	🚪	🚪

✧ Make large card pictures of other local buildings with double doors, lift-up garage doors or other unusual doors. Stick these on to a base with the drawings behind the hinged doors.
✧ Sing 'My door's a red door', on page 84.

PARTY HATS AND INVITATIONS

Objective

English – To encourage legible handwriting when giving information.

Group size

Ten to twelve children at a time.

What you need

The story, 'Tail of a peacock', on page 78, card, corrugated card, writing paper, pencils, colouring pencils or crayons, coloured papers (tissue, shiny, sticky squares and so on), adhesive, sticky tape, feathers, buttons, ribbon and party goodies (these can be either real or pretend).

Preparation

Cut the writing paper into pieces half the size of A4 to fit inside slightly larger folded pieces of card. Prepare children's name cards and invitation copy-cards, perhaps: 'Dear... , Please come to our class party at ... o'clock on Wednesday, ...th November, Love from .....'.

What to do

Read 'Tail of a peacock' and discuss the feelings we have when we're disappointed like Harry's little sister, and how the colourful peacock feather helped. Discuss party clothes and hats.

Mix up the name cards and distribute them to children to write an invitation for someone else in the group, signing it with their own name. Stick the invitations inside the cards and decorate the border and the outside.

Let the children design and make colourful party hats or crowns with the other materials, for example, from corrugated card with feathers stuck in (as shown below).

Discussion

Discuss what an invitation needs to say, the name, day, date, time, and so on. At the designated 'party' time, help the children to read out the invitations to their guests. Most children will co-operate in inviting others, but if a problem arises, ask that child to invite you, or a member of staff.

Follow-up activities

✧ Hold a small party for the children, possibly using jellies and other food. Play a game where children take turns to go into the middle of a ring with their hat on and say 'My hat is a magic hat. When I wear my hat I turn into a pilot, or a baby, or a nurse' and so on. They then make actions or noises like that character.

✧ Make a spinning top from a hexagon or octagon with a pencil through the centre. Fill in five or seven colours plus one 'rainbow' section. Spin the top. When the top stops spinning, the children whose hats are mostly the colour that rests on the ground get up and dance for the rest of the group. All dance with the rainbow.

✧ Encourage the children to write letters to members of their family who live some distance away. If possible, ask parents or guardians to supply stamped addressed envelopes so that the children can write their letters, seal them and take them to the nearest post-box or post office.

CIRCUS CLOWN

Objective

Design and Technology – To make simple mechanisms in a moving toy.

Group size

Introduce to the whole group, but carry out the activities with four to six children.

What you need

Tall Inside by Jean Richardson (Picture Puffin) or *Spot Goes to the Circus* by Eric Hill (Picture Puffin), card – white and coloured, split pins, scissors, colouring pens or crayons, ping-pong balls, modelling clay or play dough, matchsticks, thin twigs or lolly sticks, shearing elastic, the activity sheet on page 94, adhesive and spreaders or sticky tape, string.

Preparation

Cut the ping-pong balls into enough halves to give one to each child. Use the activity sheet to make cardboard templates, or prepare a photocopy for each child. Make up the two clowns as suggested in the 'What to do' section.

What to do

Read *Tall Inside* about a little girl who meets a very tall, friendly clown and becomes a clown too, or *Spot Goes to the Circus*.

Make a 'balancing clown' from the outline on the activity sheet, colouring and cutting out two little paper clowns. Stick them back to back with two matchsticks or half a lolly stick sandwiched in between. Fill the half ping-pong ball

with modelling clay and push in the clown's lolly stick or matchstick legs. The clown will wobble and right itself each time.

Colour in the templates of the large 'bigfoot clown' puppet, mount them on card and cut them out. Make the face white with a bright red nose and coloured features. Fasten the arms, legs and feet on with split pins (fairly loosely). Fasten a piece of string or shearing elastic to the head, to hold the clown up and make him dance.

Discussion

Ask the children what they would change if they could be different. Would they wish to be taller, or older? Why do clowns have red noses? Talk about what makes them laugh. Ask which parts of their body they can bend. (Children with a physical disability can show how they can move with their particular skills or aids.)

Follow-up activities

◇ Learn the poem 'Face painting' on page 72.
◇ Dramatise a story about going to the circus and becoming clowns for the day. Use PE apparatus such as mats and soft balls to practise juggling and rolling and tumbling down.
◇ Make a big wobbling clown by covering a very large balloon with papier-mâché. Paint it as a clown and put a funny hat on the top. Cut a hole in the base, weight the clown with modelling clay, and reseal.
◇ Use percussion instruments to create a circus parade of clowns, trapeze artists, jugglers and horses.
◇ Sing the song 'The clown' in *Appuskidu* (A & C Black).
◇ Learn to sing 'Middle of the ring' on page 86 of the resources section.

CANDLES AND CANDLESTICKS

Objective

RE – To increase awareness of the importance of light and colour in our lives and religious rituals.

Group size

Introduce this to the whole group, but work through the activities with four to six children.

What you need

Various candlesticks and different types of candle, such as birthday, household; white and coloured, wax tapers, nightlights, scented or shaped coloured candles, and so on. The song 'Burn, candle burn' on page 85 of the resources section.

Preparation

Darken the discussion corner by masking the windows with sugar paper or dark curtains.

What to do

Sit in the darkened corner holding hands. Discuss the children's feelings in the dark – in the group, and at home, or elsewhere. Explain that grown-ups don't like the darkness either. Light a candle and discuss their new feelings in the change from darkness to light. Continue lighting and counting candles, encouraging children from different faiths to describe their own experiences at home, church or in temple. Some children can describe the last time they had candles on their birthday cake.

Explain that all faiths value light, and that without light there would be no colours at all. Sing together the song 'Burn, candle burn'.

Discussion

As each candle is lit, the children or teacher may describe how candles are used for praise and prayer, for example: 'In some Christian churches, single candles are offered, four candles are lit in Advent; in Jewish homes and temples seven candles are lit each Sabbath and eight at the festival of Hanukkah; in Hindu and Sikh homes candles are lit at the festival of Diwali; Buddhist families use candles to celebrate Vesakha-Piya (in April or May), Guatama Buddha's birthday and the time of 'enlightenment'; Japanese Hindus put out 27 lanterns to light the way home for their ancestors' spirits.

Remind the children about the rules of safe behaviour near open flames.

Follow-up activities

✧ Make coloured layer candles as shown below.

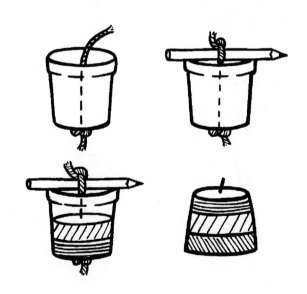

Put holes in the bases of small yoghurt pots, thread string through, knot it under the hole and tie the other end to a pencil balanced across the top. In an old saucepan slowly melt a half-and-half mixture of household candles and wax crayon stubs, one colour at a time. Pour different coloured layers into each pot while the wax is molten. Allow to cool, then cut the string at both ends and remove the pot (see below), leaving a wick at the top.
✧ Read 'Give us back the night' on page 73.

A PRESENT FOR ME?

Objective

English – To develop children's awareness of using language for information.

Group size

Introduce to the whole group, but do the activity with four to six children.

What you need

A variety of solid shaped objects, such as tins of paint, wooden bricks, long paint brushes, balls, and so on, – enough for every child to have one, with a few extra, wrapping paper, tissue paper, crêpe paper, sticky tape, ribbon, scissors, card, pencils, elastic bands, string.

Preparation

Wrap one or two objects as presents, labelling them for the group as a whole (see below). Cut big labels for writing.

What to do

Show the children a 'present' and invite them to guess what it is from the shape, feel and weight. Can they guess what it is from the colour of the wrapping paper or by reading the label? Show them the various objects which have to be wrapped up. Which will be easy to wrap – which ones more difficult?

Help children to cut, wrap and stick coloured paper around the objects, discussing choice of colour and contrasting or matching decorations.

Give each child a label to write out her or his own name and address and fasten these to pieces of string or ribbon.

Put all the presents into a big sack or bin bag and play a game in which one child at a time delivers the post, reading out the name (and address) on the label with help. Let the other children in the group guess the object inside.

Discussion

Ask the children why we wrap up gifts in colourful paper. Encourage them to help their friends by repeating their own addresses aloud when their parcels are being 'delivered'. Ask the children why it is important to remember where they live.

Follow-up activities

◇ Change the labels around for different deliveries – whose is the red parcel now?
◇ Collect used envelopes, cover the old names and addresses with sticky labels, rename and decorate for more postal deliveries.
◇ Read *Mr Rabbit and the Lovely Present* by Charlotte Zolotow (Picture Lions), about the colourful gifts for a little girl's mother.
◇ Recount the story of the Three Wise Men who brought gifts for the baby Jesus.
◇ Help the children to write letters to Santa Claus, or thank you letters to family and friends.
◇ Make up a sorting section for a home corner post office using cardboard boxes or margarine tubs to post in alphabetical order.

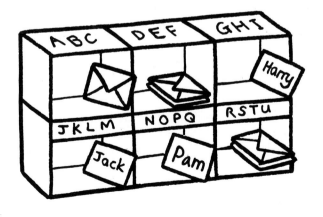

Add a few envelopes with less familiar names, such as Mr Yummy, Mrs Zebra, Miss Quiet.

FINDING YOUR WAY WITH SANTA AND RUDOLF

Objective

Geography – To reinforce understanding of 'right' and 'left' and follow directions.

Group size

All participating children.

What you need

Lots of old coloured socks and/or mittens and gloves, coloured felt pieces, glue or needles and threads, shiny red paper or red tissue paper, long and short pipe cleaners, white cotton wool.

Preparation

Make up two socks into a 'Rudolf the red-nosed reindeer' and a Santa, using felt eyes, noses and mouths, and shiny foil, rolled red tissue paper or red buttons for Rudolf's nose. Stick cotton wool whiskers, hair and beard on to the Santa sock.

Antlers can be made with pipe cleaners threaded through the socks with shorter pieces twisted round to make branches (see below).

What to do

Wear a red glove or mitten, or the Rudolf sock on your right hand and another colour on your left while you collect or greet the children, mark a register or tell a story.

Sing or say the words of 'Rudolf the red-nosed reindeer'. He was ignored by the other reindeer until one foggy night when Santa chose him to light the way with his bright red nose.

Ask the children to suggest how they could help Santa and Rudolf find their way, for example by using a torch or a map. Explain that **R**ed is for the **R**ight hand and a '**L**ovely glove' reminds you of the **L**eft hand.

Play action games, with the children taking turns to wear the Rudolf and other coloured mitten, try something like:
'Put your right hand on your head
Put your left hand on your knee'.

If time allows, let the children make their own Rudolf and Santa socks.

Discussion

Remember that children facing you will be looking at a mirror image – when you raise your right hand it will appear to be on their left-hand side. Keep your own and the children's actions separate or face in the same direction as them.

Follow-up activities

✧ Use acrylics or coloured adhesive squeezed carefully out of tubes, or thick paste and sand to create 'feely' maps.
✧ Construct floor maps with interlocking or loose bricks, modelling clay or in the sand tray, making road junctions and crossroads.
✧ Reinforce directional work with controlled buggies such as 'The Roamer' (see page 96).
✧ Encourage children to recount their experiences of getting lost and their feelings then, and when found again.
✧ Read 'Sarah and the red things', from the resources section, page 74.
✧ Sing 'Middle of the ring', on page 86 of the resources section.

STAINED GLASS WINDOWS

Objective

RE – To encourage awareness of the use of colour in religious settings.

Group size

Introduce the activity to all participating children, then work in groups of four to six.

What you need

Black sugar paper or thin card, coloured tissue paper, coloured acetates or gels if possible, coloured Cellophane (large pieces if possible or sweet wrappers), adhesive and sticky tape, scissors, Blu-Tack, two dolls or teddies from home or the home corner with three sets of clothes for each – one predominantly white, one black, and the third brightly coloured.

Preparation

Fold and cut out a black 'window frame' for each child in the group and prepare one as a stained glass window with coloured acetates (see below).

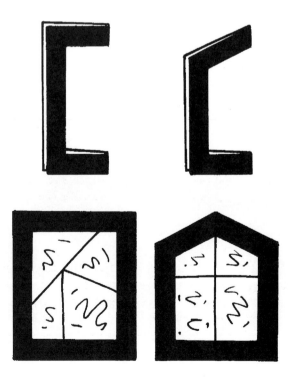

What to do

Dress the toys in white, then black, explaining they are being dressed for a special occasion. Invite suggestions as to what the special occasion might be. Repeat with the brightly coloured clothes. Guide or inform the children about ritual clothes worn for weddings, baptisms and funerals and about places of worship that are quiet and still, with colour used in special places on altars and windows, statues of prophets and saints, or on prayer shawls and prayer mats.

Tape the prepared 'stained glass' over a paper window frame and discuss the effect of the colours. Help the children to stick tissue or Cellophane over their windows, encouraging overlapping in some places and reminding them to hold them up to the light to test the effect.

Display the results by sticking them to the inside of windows.

Discussion

Two out of three children may never have visited a place of worship, so suggestions may be restricted. All ideas need to be accepted.

Discussing 'best' clothes (birthdays, visiting) will help them to relate to places of worship where special colours and clothes are worn.

Follow-up activities

✧ Cut out small window shapes to cover with coloured Cellophane sweet wrappers.
✧ Read 'In the church' on page 70.
✧ Visit a nearby place of worship and look at the colours outside and inside.
✧ Write prayers or poems about the family and decorate them as in holy books, using silver and gold crayons to make a picture, or a border with a repeat pattern of the alphabet (the Qur'an has no pictures but uses the Arabic script in its art and design).

CHAPTER 6
WEATHER

Weather has an enormous impact on our lives, influencing our moods and behaviour. Old sayings like, 'Red sky at night... sailor's (or shepherd's) delight', show how we interpret the weather through colour and other factors. This chapter looks at rainbows and snowflakes, seasonal changes and colours at night.

FINDING RAINBOWS

Objective

Music – To compose music to accompany a story and create musical effects.

Group size

The whole group.

What you need

The Ladybird Bible Storybook for the story of Noah and a rainbow picture, enough musical instruments to have one for each child, the song 'A rainbow world' on page 87.

Preparation

None.

What to do

Read the story of Noah, who takes the animals into the Ark. God sends a rainbow as a promise that he will never send another flood.

Look at the picture of the rainbow and discuss the colours and the shape. Use the instruments to suggest different animals marching into the Ark, individual animals at first, then keeping in time together – 1, 2, 1, 2... use coconuts for horses, drums for elephants, kazoos for mosquitoes and so on. Make little tapping noises for raindrops, just one or two drops at first, then faster and louder – use cymbals and drums for thunder. Let the children suggest sounds for the watery waves and the diminishing flood. Help them to select sounds for each colour of the rainbow at the end. Retell the story with the musical accompaniment, then sing 'A rainbow world', on page 87.

Discussion

Discuss the children's experiences of rainbows, storms and flooding – at home or in the street.

Rainbows occur because of the way light rays behave within the raindrops still in the air. Indigo and violet are not easy to identify – 'purple' and 'pink' can indicate a 'bluish-purple' and a 'reddish-purple' – near enough to satisfy.

Follow-up activities

◇ Accompany the songs 'Sing a rainbow' in *Apusskidu* (A & C Black) and 'Up above, down below' in the resources section, page 80.
◇ Make a rainbow bubble mixture using three parts water to one part good quality detergent. Make bubble blowers from washing-up liquid bottles (as shown below). Dip into the bubble mixture and blow gently. Observe the rainbow colours and the reflections.

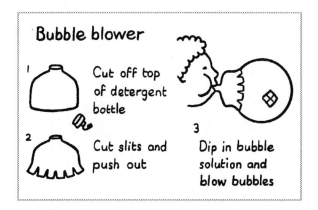

Bubble blower

1 Cut off top of detergent bottle

2 Cut slits and push out

3 Dip in bubble solution and blow bubbles

◇ Make coloured spinning tops from circles of strong or double card (see the activity sheet on page 93) using a pencil through the centre as the vertical stem to spin on.
◇ Read the story 'Roy, the hat boy' on page 76.
◇ Read the poems 'The rainbow', 'Sun, sun', and 'I'm glad', all on page 70.

RAINBOW DAYS

Objective

History – To develop a knowledge of the passage of time, using days of the week.

Group size

Four to seven children.

What you need

Card, the activity sheet on page 95, string or laces, coloured crayons or similar.

Preparation

Use the photocopiable activity sheet to cut seven overlapping pages, cut down the middle and punched for strings or laces (as shown below). Write the days of the week in the colours of the rainbow, Monday in red, Tuesday in orange, and so on (as shown). Prepare one set for each child.

What to do

Mix up the pieces on the table and ask the children to put the 'jigsaw' together. When all the pieces are in place, play a guessing game by removing or covering up one of the 'day' pieces.

Turn the pages while saying the following rhyme (or use children's personal details):

> On Monday night the moon (or stars) was bright;
> On Tuesday morning my dog / Dad / cat was snoring;
> On Wednesday my friend (name) came to play;
> On Thursday early (late) my hair went curly (straight);
> On Friday at tea there was cake (honey) for me;
> On Saturday Grandma (Uncle) came to stay;
> On Sunday afternoon, we all played a tune;
> And Sunday's the end..... So we all start again........

Let the children colour in or draw two matching pictures on each side of the day before fastening the pieces together with string or laces to make matching pages in the Rainbow Book.

Discussion

Ask the children to explain how they know which pieces will match (by the colour or shape of the arch). Encourage them to feel along the edges of the first curved pages. Discuss the days of the week and their order and pattern.

Follow-up activities

✧ Make a big daily diary with sugar paper or A3 pages recording positive events and individual achievements, such as 'Monday: Today we all made scones. Raja wrote his name. Melanie helped Sara.'
✧ Sing 'Up above, down below', on page 80 of the resources section.
✧ Focus on arches in the children's construction work – making arches with loose and interlocking bricks and everyday materials in models.
✧ Do an arched dance, such as 'Strip the willow'. Use Scottish dance music or sing 'The grand old Duke of York'. Children (in yellow bands) face partners (blue bands) in a line. The first pair hold both hands and skip between the lines of children to the end, then skip back again.
  The first pair then separate, turn outwards, and lead their own line in a follow-my-leader down the room until they meet again. They join hands to form an arch and the two lines of children pair up again as they go underneath to reform a line with a new 'first pair' at the top.

I CAN FEEL THE WIND

Objective

Music – To encourage awareness of high and low pitch in sounds and music.

Group size

All participating children.

What you need

Various musical instruments, preferably some with variable pitch and notes such as 'plunge whistles', kazoos or recorders and xylophones, hairdryer or vacuum cleaner, card and a big piece of cloth.

Preparation

Take a length of card and paint blocks of rainbow colours on one side from red through to orange, yellow and green to blue.

What to do

Go outside to feel the wind or use the large cloth to flap the air in front of the children and ask them what they can feel. Make a wind sound 'oooOOOOOOOOOOOooo' starting low, rising, then falling again.

Ask the children to help you with the wind, rising and falling with hands as well as voices, reaching high or crouching low.

Hold the colour card vertically and start by singing a fairly high note for red while you travel down the card and the scale with finger and voice to blue. Do this alone first, then try it with the children.

Use the instruments to play the lowest, then the highest notes the children can find. If you have a hairdryer or vacuum cleaner switch it on and listen to the changes in the sound at different speeds.

Discussion

Ask the children if they can hear any differences in the wind. Emphasise the change in pitch by adding a slight whistling sound if possible.

Very young children often confuse loudness and pitch, but physical emphasis on 'going up' or 'down' can actually help.

Follow-up activities

✧ Play or sing songs with clear rising and falling notes such as 'Lavender's blue' or 'The grand old Duke of York'.
✧ Make coloured poems by writing high words at the top in red (for example aeroplane, bird, chimney pot) down to blue or purple words at the base of the poem (for example floor, beetles, underground). Read them with the children changing the pitch of your voice for high and low words.
✧ Make fans – colour pieces of paper, fold into concertina shapes and secure the ends with sticky tape. Use the fans to make and feel the wind.
✧ Look at wind instruments, and use them in 'Oh, we can play on the big bass drum' and 'The music man' in *Okki-Tokki-Unga* (A & C Black) and 'It's noisy' in Scholastic Collections, *Songs*.
✧ Make stairs for reading in sequence (and pitch), as shown here.

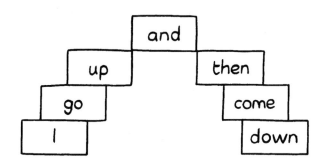

DANCE WITH THE WIND

Objective

PE – To develop control and co-ordination.

Group size

The whole group.

What you need

Coloured crêpe paper, tissue and newspaper, ribbons if available, old or spare paint brushes, sticky tape, a few dead leaves or paper ones, a cassette of pleasant music and a cassette recorder, poem 'The autumn leaves' on page 69.

Preparation

Cut 50 cm lengths of crêpe and tissue paper or newspaper about 8 cm wide (and some lengths of ribbon about the same length). Attach some of the tissue or newspaper strips to the ends of brushes with sticky tape (to swirl as they wave). Make one or two longer streamers (about one metre in length) for yourself.

What to do

If it is autumn, go out for a walk to watch the leaves fall, or throw the dried leaves in the air a few times, and encourage pupils to look at and talk about their movement. Ask the children to simulate the leaf movements in the wind with the hand-held crêpe streamers, standing still in spaces, then moving carefully around the room to music. Repeat this with the tissue or newspaper streamers and ribbons, discussing any differences.

Use the streamers in dances as follows:

Divide the children into two groups and show each group certain movements. One group become the 'cocoas', the others are 'beamers'. The 'cocoas' circle their streamers to their left and around (in the shape of the letters c, a and o) while the 'beamers' make downward vertical movements, then up and over (in the shape of b, h, m and n).

Swap movements, then take turns in pairs to dance around a partner as a 'cocoa' or a 'beamer'. Finish with the poem 'The autumn leaves', throwing the hand-held streamers in the air a few times and crouching down while they fall.

Discussion

Ask the children if they think of anything else when they see the coloured streamers swishing or waving in the air (possibly waves on the sea, flags or fireworks).

Follow-up activities

✧ Use the children's suggestions of movements or other letters (s, x, w) to compose a short dance sequence in groups. Show this to other members of the group or use it for a Sharing Assembly.

✧ Get some party streamers and watch how they unravel when thrown, measuring them with footsteps.

✧ Read and dramatise the story of the argument between the Sun and the Wind as to who was the more powerful. The Wind failed the challenge to 'blow' the coat off the traveller, while the hot Sun succeeded with 'warm persuasion'!

✧ Make and colour paper spirals and hang them from threads at their centres over a radiator or floor heating where the warm air rising will make them spin.

✧ Sing 'Middle of the ring' on page 86 of the resources section.

SNOWFLAKES AND RAINDROPS

Objective

Mathematics – To develop knowledge of shapes and their properties, in particular triangles, circles and hexagons.

Group size

Introduce to all participating children, but work through the activity with four to six children.

What you need

Card templates or big plastic plane shapes, especially circles, triangles and hexagons, white paper, transparent material such as plastic packaging (possibly greetings card box lids), white cotton thread, scissors, a small bowl of water, sticky tape.

Preparation

For younger children, prepare some paper circles ready folded over, first in half, then in thirds.

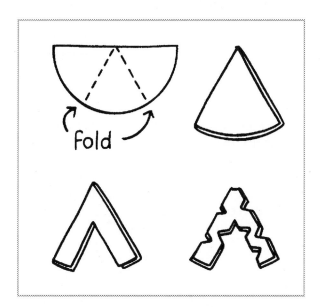

Fold

What to do

Ask the children to describe the 'colour' of snow or rain. Show *white* paper, and dip your hand into water to show the 'drops' on the ends of your fingers. Ask the children to describe the 'colour' of these, and the shape of the drops, and compare their suggestions with the plane shapes.

Show different (regular) shapes such as squares or circles by folding in half, in half again, and so on.

Then ask the children to describe the new shapes made by folding.

For six-sided snowflakes, fold circles in half, then in thirds (as shown). Cut this into two 'legs', then cut small pieces from either side and open out. For raindrops, cut out transparent triangles, slightly curved on the bottom corners. Hang snowflakes and raindrops from the ceiling, stringing three or four on a piece of thread, varying the levels between drops or flakes.

Discussion

Children may not be familiar with the vocabulary or concept of 'see-through' or 'transparent' and may say that rain is white. If this is the case ask if they can think of anything that is see-through.

Follow-up activities

✧ Draw round plane shapes on to sticky coloured squares, cut out the shapes and use them to make pictures or patterns.
✧ Leave a dish of water in a warm place or on the window-sill and watch what happens to the level of water in the dish. If some condenses again on the window ask the children to explain how the water got there.
✧ Do water paintings on white sugar paper or on the playground or any safe paved area. Choose a warm day, and use pots of clean water and brushes only. Time how long it takes for the water paintings to disappear.
✧ Read the poems 'Winter morning' and 'Overnight' both on page 73.
✧ Sing 'Up above, down below' (page 80).

SPINNING RAINBOWS

Objective

Art – To explore colour matching and mixing, especially the primary colours.

Group size

Four to six children at a time.

What you need

The photocopiable activity sheet of circles with patterns (page 93), 'wet' paint and dry powder paint, eight to twelve saucers or shallow dishes, spoons, felt-tipped pens or crayons, scissors, short stubby pencils, card, plastic spatulas or brushes, adhesive.

Preparation

Make up quantities of red, yellow and blue paint. Make a photocopy of the activity sheet for each child. Cut enough pieces of card to match the circles pages. Cut out four to six of the patterned circles, stick them on to card and push pencil stubs through the centre.

What to do

Let the children put spoonfuls of wet red paint into their saucers. Ask them to predict the effect of adding yellow paint, then give each child different amounts of yellow. Stir with a spatula or brush and discuss the results.

Repeat the exercise with spoonfuls of dry red and yellow powder paint. Repeat with these or other children, mixing yellow with blue and blue with red. Use the paints to colour the spinning tops.

Show the children the prepared 'blank' spinning tops and how to spin them. Use one of the prepared paints (or crayon, etc) to colour one part of the top and predict the effect when spinning. Repeat with another colour, predicting and spinning. Discuss the effects of mixing colours. Let the children colour other circles, stick these to a card backing and cut out. Push stubby pencils through the middles and spin.

Discussion

Ask the children 'What does this colour remind you of?' and 'Can you see anything else in the room the same colour as this?'.

Follow-up activities

✧ Use some blank spinning tops with wet paint. Make sure children wear overalls, and stand around a deep tray. Spin a top in the tray and pour a spoonful of wet paint on to it while it is spinning. What pattern is made on the cardboard top?

✧ Mix some prepared wallpaper paste with coloured wet paint and use large spoonfuls of this on a smooth surface for hand painting, mixing colours and making prints.

✧ Use electricity kits (suitable for young children) to fasten the coloured circles on to motors and spin them that way.

✧ Read 'Painting' and 'Fingerpaints' on page 72 of the resources section.

✧ Sing 'Colour splash' on page 83.

UMBRELLA COLOUR

Objective

History – To encourage an awareness of the passage of time and stories of the past.

Group size

All the children.

What you need

A colourful umbrella, a large piece of card, large felt-tipped pens, scissors, split pins, paper, pencils.

Preparation

Cut out a large circle of card roughly 50 cm in diameter. Divide it into eight sections, curve the edges between the points into an umbrella shape and fasten a cardboard 'clock-hand' at the centre with a split pin. Write the days of the week in seven different colours in seven sections with the question 'What was the weather like on ...?' on the last section in black.

[Illustration: umbrella-shaped diagram divided into eight sections labelled Sunday, What was the weather like on, Monday, Tuesday, Wednesday, Thursday, Friday, Saturday, with a clock-hand at the centre]

What to do

Discuss the magic 'flying' umbrella that belonged to the unusual Nanny, Mary Poppins, who flew two children above London to see the sights.

Initiate discussion with this story or make up a story of your own, showing your colourful umbrella and explaining that it likes to play with the wind, for example:

'One windy Monday, the wind blew the umbrella up above the tree tops. On a rainy Tuesday the umbrella came down into a field. Wednesday was stormy and the umbrella flew out to sea. Thursday was sunny and breezy and the umbrella landed on a beach. Friday... (and so on), until the umbrella flew back home again.'

Retell the story, using the card umbrella, and write or draw in the weather for that day. Keep a simple record of the weather over a week writing the details in colour to match the day colour.

Discussion

Ask the children to imagine what Mary Poppins or the umbrella could see from high up on Monday, Tuesday and so on. What effect would the weather have on the flying trips? What colours are there in the weather?

Follow-up activities

✧ After one week's complete record, the children can spin the clock-hand on the umbrella and write a sentence about the day they get, such as 'On Monday it was raining', adding drawings of clothes in the colour of the day and writing about what they did on that day.

✧ Bring in a selection of umbrellas and encourage the children to look at colours, patterns and handles – use these for sorting and discussion.

✧ Read the action poem 'The autumn leaves' on page 69 of the resources section.

✧ Sing 'The weather-or nots' and 'Lots of weather' in Scholastic Collections, *Songs*.

✧ Make 'windballs' by cutting and colouring several paper circles (about 12–15 cm in diameter). Stick five or six together at the centres, back to back to make the surfaces curved inwards. Release them in the playground or another open area on a windy day and measure how far they tumble.

COLOUR AT NIGHT

Objective

Art – To record experiences of night and darkness and develop a sense of perspective.

Group size

Introduce to the whole group, prepare the artwork with four to six children.

What you need

Tom and Pippo See the Moon by Helen Oxenbury (Walker), black and white sugar paper, white and black paint, chalk, charcoal, coloured wax crayons or pastels, masking tape, old brushes, coloured sticky paper squares or coloured tissue paper, glue sticks, scissors, diffusers; poem 'Give us back the night' on page 73 of the resources section.

Preparation

Fold a piece of white sugar paper in half, then fold vertically again. Cut squares out of the second fold to produce an E-shape that opens out into a 'window frame'. Use sticky tape to fasten this over a sheet of black paper to suggest a window 'at night' (see below).

What to do

Read about the little boy, Tom, who sees the moon shining in the darkness and is told about rockets going to the moon. Show the 'window at night' and ask the children to suggest what they might see if they looked out of this window. Read 'Give us back the night' to encourage further suggestions.

Use the black sugar paper and white paint to paint stars in the sky, using diffusers or spots of paint, or (if space allows) flick the paint across the paper in spatters. Paint in a big yellow moon. When the paint dries add extra objects in crayons or pastels. Cut out houses or rocket ships from coloured paper, and add these. Finally, stick the white sugar paper window frames over the front.

Discussion

Ask the children to suggest what makes it dark at night and how lights can stop people from being afraid. What colour are the street lights? The lights from the houses? Children in an urban environment will have less experience of the stars as street lighting and pollution can obscure the view.

Follow-up activities

✧ Choose a dark day and stand outside to look at the lights on in the buildings around you.
✧ Make a 'Night Sights' display (see page 61), and put the children's window pictures nearby.
✧ Do wax resist paintings. Use thick, coloured wax crayons on good quality white paper to draw bonfires, fireworks, rocketships or stars. Paint over with black staining ink (if possible) or thin black water paint.
✧ Use white chalk or paint on black paper, or black charcoal on white paper, for other pictures of the night sky.
✧ Make a collage on coloured card using varieties and textures of black and white fabrics only.
✧ Sing 'Twinkle, twinkle, little star' and 'God who put the stars in space' in *Someone's Singing, Lord* (A & C Black).
✧ Make rocket ships to suspend from the ceiling from kitchen roll tubes or poster tubes, covered with shiny kitchen foil or paint (acrylic paints are very effective for this).
✧ Using a strong torch or overhead projector to shine on the children's profiles, draw and cut out their silhouettes in black or white paper mounting them on the opposite for contrast.

CHAPTER 7
DISPLAYS

This chapter offers a number of display ideas which relate to the theme of Colours. Some of these suggestions are linked to individual activities while others can be used in a more general way.

Children should be involved in the preparation and development of the displays whenever possible — sponge-painting the backdrop, constructing models and bringing objects from home. They should be encouraged to try out their own display ideas and discuss the results of their efforts. A display can often change and grow as it stimulates further responses from the children.

WHAT'S ON FIRE?

What you need

Black cloth or paper, art media, papier mâché.

Preparation

Make a large cone shape of card (approximately 30cm high) and fix it to a base or tray to make a volcano. Cut out a large card sun (approximately 1m in diameter) with flames around the edges. Cover the display board and table-top in black.

What to do

Let the children colour the sun thickly with red, orange and yellow paint, using brushes and water paints, rollers with acrylic paint or scrunched up tissue paper. Fasten the sun to the backdrop.

Papier mâché the cone, leaving the surface rough. Allow to dry, then paint with greys and browns until half-way up, finishing with dark and bright reds. Add brightly coloured paper strips to

the top for flames and molten lava. Spread a little paste around the base and sprinkle on sand and small pebbles.

Discussion

Ask the children what it would be like if the sun stopped shining. Explain that the sun's fire keeps things alive, gives us light and makes all the colours in the world.

Ideas to extend the display

✧ Display real sunflowers or marigolds, if in season, for the children to observe, draw or paint, or use an illustration of Van Gogh's 'Sunflowers' to stimulate artwork and language.

✧ Observe, then make models of candles with rolls of card, and flames of tissue paper.

✧ Write out and display the poems 'I like colours', 'Sun, sun', and 'What's yellow, then?' on pages 69, 70 and 71 of the resources section.

RAINBOW COLOURS

What you need

Light-coloured backing paper or cloth, paints and brushes, coloured fabrics, objects and art materials, in colours to match each display.

Preparation

Draw arched lines on the backing paper and let the children paint in the rainbow colours. For a changing six-week display, cover the table-top in red and orange for weeks 1 and 2, then yellow and green for weeks 3 and 4, finishing with blue and purple for weeks 5 and 6.

What to do

Make paintings, patterns and textured collages using paper, fabric, buttons, and string dipped in relevant colours to match those currently on display, for example, red and orange: volcanoes, oranges, fire engines; yellow and green: sunshine, apples, lizards; blue and purple: under the ocean, a thunderstorm, blackberries, night-time. Draw around one boy and one girl from the group and cut the figures out. Draw and cut out clothes to fit, and paint these in the relevant colours — red and orange party clothes, yellow and green summer clothes, blue and purple rainy day clothes. Change the clothes each fortnight.

Discussion

Ask the children if all red (or the week's colour) things are exactly the same. Encourage the use of vocabulary such as 'dark red', 'pale', 'pinkish-red', or 'reddish-orange'. Let the children display any clothes they are wearing that match the current display in some way.

Ideas to extend the display

✧ Add matching vocabulary words such as red, run, rip, rat; orange, on, over, of; adjectives and similes, both established or thought up by the children such as butter yellow; sunny yellow; sky blue; as green as grass; he was blue with cold; as blue as my big ball.

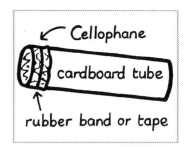

✧ Display models made from recycled materials, construction kits and modelling clay to match the two current rainbow colours, for example cars and lorries; an orange house; snakes; pots and beads. Attach coloured streamers from the rainbow down to the objects to reinforce the position of those colours in the rainbow.

✧ Make matching viewing telescopes from kitchen roll tubes with Cellophane or filters fastened over the ends.

✧ Display items such as flowers and fruit, jams and jellies, umbrellas and balloons to match the colours of the week.

Rainbow colours

red
orange
yellow
green
blue
indigo
violet

red things

orange things

My cat

orange hat

NIGHT SIGHTS

What you need

Dark blue paper or cloth, sponges, art materials, especially black sugar paper, square and rectangular blocks for printing.

Preparation

Cut out tall blocks of flats and/or houses in black sugar paper to match your local buildings. Draw windows on in pencil. Cut templates of cars (use the activity sheets on pages 92 and 93 for bodies and wheels).

What to do

Darken the backing paper a little further with sponges and dark bluish-grey paint. Let the children block-print the windows of their buildings in white, cream or yellow, allow the buildings to dry, then arrange them on the backing paper to represent a village, city or town. Use paint, crayons, coloured sticky paper and so on to create pictures of shop front windows such as dress shops, toy shops, shoe shops or fast-food restaurants. Attach these at the base of the display in front of the buildings with lit windows. Let the children draw around and cut out the car shapes in dark coloured paper and add white front lights or red rear lights in bright paint, sticky paper or shiny foil. Add bright blue or red lights on the top of some cars for a police or a fire chief's car.

Paint tall dark lamp-posts and traffic lights, then use thick, brightly-coloured paints or shiny foil to create their bright lights. Cut these out and pin them to the backdrop.

Discussion

Ask the children to suggest why it gets dark at night. What can they see when they look out into the dark? Can they guess why the cars have different colours at the front and the back? Do they know what the different traffic light colours tell the drivers to do?

Ideas to extend the display

✧ Put torches on the display table and cover the lights in coloured Cellophane to explore the effect of coloured lights.

✧ Restrict the painting colours to purples, dark blues and blacks to make patterns or pictures.

✧ Let the children use thick soft black pencils and charcoal for their drawings.

✧ Add vocabulary to inspire poems about the night – dark, lights, shine, sky, bed, sleep – and words beginning with 'n', such as no, not, nice, now, never, nip, none.

✧ Draw pictures of people who work at night (especially parents or guardians) – police, nurses, disc jockeys, bus drivers and so on.

✧ Write out and display the poem 'Give us back the night', on page 73.

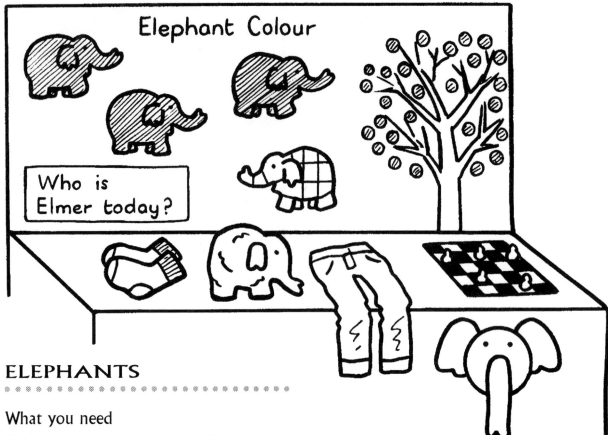

ELEPHANTS

What you need

Cream or pale sand-coloured backing paper or cloth, brown, green and grey paint, brushes, corks, pinboard and drawing pins or staples, the elephants made by the children from the 'Elephant colours' activity on page 22.

Preparation

Prepare a background area which is large enough to hold all the children's elephants and cover it with pale-coloured paper.

What to do

Paint a big tree with grey, cork-printed berries down one side of the display or paint it on to sugar paper, then cut it out and pin it on.

Pin the children's elephants in a herd with the grey colour showing. Choose one child to have her or his Elmer colours showing. Change the display each day to select a different child's brightly coloured elephant.

Discussion

Ask the children to guess each day whose special elephant is on display before you say the name.

Even if the name shows a little, this will encourage observation, prediction and self-esteem.

Ask the children which direction the grey elephants are facing. What about the Elmer elephant?

Ideas to extend the display

✧ Add a question to the display such as 'Who is Elmer today?'
✧ Add vocabulary like elephant, trunk, colour, grey, tall, berries, tail, herd; or try elephant, egg, every, Elmer, elderberry, end, eat, eaten, easy.
✧ Make and wall mount a front or rear view picture of an elephant and cut out a separate trunk or tail. Stick a small piece of folded masking tape to the trunk (or tail) and play a 'stick the trunk on' game with the children blindfolded, or with eyes closed, guessing the place to stick the trunk.
✧ Use everyday materials or construction kits to make models of elephants for a table-top display.
✧ Collect items to display that are predominantly grey, for example Dad's socks, school trousers, cardigans, and so on.
✧ Use black and white modelling clay to make little shapes, animals or people. Display them standing on a draughts or chess board.

THE RAIN FOREST

What you need

Green cloth or paper, corrugated card, sponges, green party streamers, crêpe paper, leaves, art and craft media.

Preparation

Cut two large tree trunks with smaller branches from the corrugated card. Cover the table-top with green or brown cloth or paper.

What to do

Darken areas of the backdrop cloth or paper with darker greens sponged on by the children.

Paint the tree trunks and branches brown and fix these on either side of the backdrop, with the branches overlapping across the display. Make rubbings or paint prints from the leaves, cut them out and fasten on to the branches. Unravel some green party streamers, drape and pin over the display to give a tangled creeper effect. Add a variety of painted or paper flowers, butterflies, insects and birds in bright colours, amongst the branches and on the table-top.

Discussion

Ask the children to describe any trees they are familiar with in their gardens and streets, in the playground or local woods. Explain that the trees help to make the air around us good to breathe and provide a home for lots of living things. Ask what they think might happen if all the trees were cut down.

Ideas to extend the display

✧ Make models of unusual or fantastical animals using clay, recycled materials or construction kits for the table-top display, perhaps a chameleon, a tree frog, or giant spiders.
✧ Display pots with ferns and other indoor plants with interesting green foliage, describe the shapes and look for spores under the fern leaves.
✧ Write out and display the poem 'Green song' on page 71 of the resources section.
✧ Learn the song 'Green green green', on page 81 of the resources section.

fun
find
forest

What is it like
in the dark
dark woods?

CHAPTER 8
ASSEMBLIES

This chapter suggests ideas for assemblies or group sharing times all based on the theme of Colours. Where possible, they reflect the experiences that the children will have had in carrying out the activities elsewhere in this book.

COLOURS IN THE NATURAL WORLD

This assembly asks the children to draw on earlier experiences, particularly in art work, colour-sorting tasks and observations of colours in the natural world. These activities should have heightened their awareness of the rich selection of colours to be found in their immediate environment and beyond, helping them to reflect upon the beauty and variety around them.

The assembly will work in a range of settings, and is suitable for a large gathering or with a smaller group; if the weather is suitable, it could even take place outside!

Introduction

The person leading the assembly should begin by helping the children to focus on the work they have already done on colour – perhaps asking some of them to show their paintings using different shades of blue, their collection of things that are red or to read their poems about yellow.

Activity

Children dressed to represent different colours (perhaps the colours of the rainbow) should be invited to come forward and members of the audience called upon to identify their colours.

If the group is small, the other children can spend a few moments finding things around them to 'match' with the colours represented by their peers. In a larger group gathering, it might be more appropriate to

ask for suggestions instead of the items themselves! This activity should help the children to establish that their world is rich in colours of many different shades and forms.

Reflection

The leader should encourage all the children to think about the colours they have seen and to choose their favourite. Remind the children that although they may have a favourite, the world is beautiful because of the wide range of colours.

While the children in the audience reflect on this for a few moments, the children representing the various colours can dance and move together, showing how colours complement and contrast with one another. Use appropriate background music and the children can carry coloured streamers to twist and twirl as they dance.

Prayer

Some children may like the opportunity to praise and thank God for creating a world that is full of such beauty and may want to express their gratitude at being able to enjoy colours. The children may wish to compose their own prayers or the leader might choose one from an anthology.

Song

The song 'A Rainbow World' on page 87 of the resources section is suitable to use with this assembly. It reflects the theme of the assembly without being specifically religious in any way.

COLOURS OF THE SEASONS

In this country, different colours often seem to be linked with particular seasons in the year. In spring, many trees and plants display fresh green foliage and children may also be aware of bright yellow daffodils and the vivid pinks and reds of other flowers, especially if they have planted the bulbs themselves. Summer is a time for warm colours, like the golden yellow of the sun in a clear blue sky as well as the brilliant colours of the seaside. In autumn, children may notice how fruit and field crops grow ripe, while the leaves change to russet, orange and brown. Winter is a time of sparkling frosts and maybe even snow, while Christmas brings the evergreens with shining red berries. The focus could be on all four seasons or just one, appropriate to the time of year.

This assembly would be suitable for use in a variety of settings, including a large school or nursery or with a much smaller playgroup.

Introduction

The person leading the assembly should begin by reminding the children of previous activities which link with the season(s) chosen and the results of these could be shared with everyone, for example bulbs that are in bloom, paintings of the sun (shading from yellow to red using colour mixing techniques), collages of autumn leaves or snowflakes cut from white paper decorated with silver glitter.

The leader should go on to invite the children to recall other examples of colours associated with the particular time(s) of the year.

Activity

Children could depict the chosen season(s) through movement and/or dance, dressed in appropriate colours, costumes or masks. They could represent flowers pushing up through the earth and bursting into bloom, the warm rays of the sun reaching out to everyone, autumn leaves twirling down from the trees or snowflakes falling in gentle spirals to the ground. Appropriate music would enhance this activity — Vivaldi's 'Four Seasons' is a good choice!

Reflection

The leader should invite the children to look at the colours before them and to reflect on the seasons connected with them. Children might like to think of times in their own experience when they have been aware of the atmosphere and colours of a particular season. This could be accompanied by music or the use of coloured lighting. In a smaller group it would be possible for children to have an opportunity to share their reflections if they wish to do so.

Prayer

It may be appropriate to invite some children to share in a prayer about the beauty of seasonal colours and to thank God for them. This could be structured to include the thoughts and prayers of some of the children themselves.

Song

This could be chosen to link with the current season — for example, a gathering which focuses on winter might be enhanced by the theme from the Raymond Briggs film 'The Snowman' or Tchaikovsky's 'Dance of the Sugar Plum Fairy' from 'The Nutcracker Suite'.

HOW DO COLOURS MAKE US FEEL?

This assembly encourages children to reflect upon the way in which colour is used to enhance or reinforce feelings or emotions and how colours are used as symbols in the world around us.

Introduction

The person leading the assembly should begin by asking the children to think about activities they have done which look at the meaning of different colours – these might have included the traffic light game where red means 'stop', amber means 'get ready' and green means 'go'; or a task which focuses on the blue and red symbols which appear on taps and so on.

Activity

Different colours should be introduced using large pieces of fabric and/or coloured lighting. As each colour is shown, children can be invited to give descriptions of it and show models and pictures of examples of how it is used to convey meaning.

For example, red is a bright colour which acts as a warning or signal – fire engines are red so that they can be seen easily and so too are post-boxes; silver and gold are bright, shiny and expensive and denote that something is special and important – tinsel shows that Christmas is a particularly special, happy time of year.

Reflection

Children might like to reflect on feelings evoked by various colours and a range of musical moods could be included to complement this. The leader might like to guide the children in this, particularly if they are very young. In a smaller group, children could be invited to share their reflections.

Prayer

Children could be invited to share in a prayer about the wonderful colours in their world which help to make it such a stimulating and exciting place to be.

Song

Any song which features colours would be appropriate here; alternatively, a piece of music which reflects the mood of one of the colours chosen could be played as the children disperse.

Collective worship in schools

The assemblies outlined here are suitable for use with children in nurseries and playgroups, but would need to be adapted for use with pupils registered in schools. As a result of legislation enacted in 1944, 1988 and 1993, there are now specific points to be observed when developing a programme of Collective Acts of Worship in a school.

Further guidance will be available from your local SACRE – Standing Advisory Council for R.E.

ACTION RHYMES AND POEMS

COLOUR COUNTING

Starting with the thumb, stick a coloured paper circle on each nail:
red, blue, yellow, white, green.

Begin with the hand held up, palm away from the face. As the
rhyme is said, bend the finger away from yourself to make it
disappear.

Red – blue – yellow – white and green,
(Wriggle each one as the colour is said)

The funniest fingers you have ever seen.
(Wriggle them all)
1–2–3–4–5.
All my fingers are alive!
(Continue wriggling)
But, Mr Red –
went to bed.
(Bend 'red' finger)
Mr Blue –
went there too.
(Bend 'blue' finger)
Now I've only three.
Mr Yellow –
said 'Hello'
(Bend 'yellow' finger)
Now I've only two.
Mr White –
had a fright.
(Bend 'white' finger)
Now I've only one.
Mr Green –
couldn't be seen.
(Bend 'green' finger)
Now – there's – none – at – all!

Delphine Evans

MY WINDOW-BOX

*Use one hand as the window-box, and the fingers of the other hand
to represent the bulbs, the watering-can and the growing flowers.
Children can suggest alternative colours for flowers.*

I planted one bulb
in my window-box,
and watered it every day.
So now all my friends
see a bright red flower,
when they come round to play.

I planted two bulbs
in my window-box,
and watered them every day.
So now all my friends
see two bright red flowers,
when they come round to play.

I planted three bulbs, etc.

I planted four bulbs, etc.

I planted five bulbs, etc.

Linda Hammond

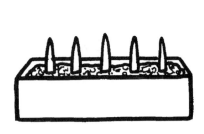

IN GRAN'S JEWELLERY BOX

*Hold up seven fingers for the first items in the jewellery box. Lower
hands, then hold up six fingers. Then five, and so on. Use the hands
to make a box shape at the close of the poem.*

In my Gran's jewellery box
I found
Seven silver bracelets,
Six emerald earrings,
Five yellow brooches,
Four gold necklaces,
Three ruby rings,
Two sky-blue lockets,
And one brown pocket watch
That ticks and tocks.
And that's what I found
In my Gran's jewellery box.

Wes Magee

THE AUTUMN LEAVES

Raise hands. Move them slowly down, with fingers waggling, at every 'Down' in verse 1.

Repeat actions for verse 2. ('Colours' replace 'Down' words).

In autumn
The trees wave in the wind
And the leaves come tumbling
Down,
Down,
Down
And
Down.

Here they come,
Hundreds and thousands of leaves,
In Yellow, Red,
Hazel,
Gold
And
Chocolate
Brown.

Wes Magee

I LIKE COLOURS

I like blue.
I like the sky
where birds fly high.

I like yellow.
I like the sun
when we have fun.

I like green.
I like frogs
as still as logs.

I like black.
I like the dark
when foxes bark.

Pie Corbett

THE RAINBOW

The rainbow's like a coloured bridge
that sometimes shines from ridge to ridge.
Today one end is in the sea,
the other's in the field with me.

Iain Crichton Smith

SUN, SUN

'Sun, Sun overhead,
What's your colour?'

'I am red.'

'Sun, Sun, fiery fellow,
What's your colour?'

'I am yellow.'

'Sun, Sun in sky of blue,
What's your colour?'

'Orange too.
I'm golden yellow,
Orange and red,
A burning fire above your head.'

Robert Heidbreder

I'M GLAD

I'm glad the sky is painted blue,
And earth is painted green,
With such a lot of nice fresh air
All sandwiched in between.

Anon.

IN THE CHURCH

See the colours
In the stained-glass window.
See orange, green,
Pink, purple,
Yellow, brown
And blue.

See how the colours
In the stained-glass window glow
When the sun's red rays
Come shining,
Shining, shining
Through.

Wes Magee

GREEN SONG

Trees are green
and peas are green
but what's the very
greenest green?

A runner bean
and knees are green
when rolling in the grass
they've been.

A caterpillar's
nose is green,
seaweed between
your toes is green.

A frog beneath
his log is green,
a thick pea-soupy
fog is green.

A nettle's green,
an apple's green,
a mouldy cheese
is old and green
but what's the very
greenest green
of all the greens
that you have seen?

Judith Nicholls

WHAT'S YELLOW THEN?

A dandelion, a buttercup, a sunflower,
the middle of a daisy, if you please.
Mustard, custard,
pumpkin, peach and popcorn –
and a great big lump
of smelly yellow cheese!

Judith Nicholls

PHOTOCOPIABLE RESOURCES

PAINTING

There's red paint on my hands,
(Wipe hands together)
and green paint in my hair.
(Stroke hair with both hands)
There's blue paint on my nose,
(Touch nose)
but I don't really care!

There's black paint on my shirt,
(Wipe hands down front)
and yellow on my shoes.
(Touch shoes)
There's so much paint on me,
(Point to self)
there's no more paint to use!

Linda Hammond

FINGERPAINTS

Take a dab of yellow.
Pick a bit of blue.
Mix them on the table
to a thick green goo.

Sketch a red sailboat.
Splotch a yellow sun.
Swirl around your fingertips.
Fingerpaints are fun!

Tony Mitton

FACE PAINTING

Shall I be a badger,
shall I be a clown?
Shall I be a cross-patch
with a nasty frown?

Shall I be an old man,
wrinkles on my skin?
Or shall I be a baby
with dimples on my
bottom?

Judith Nicholls

GIVE US BACK THE NIGHT

When the sun goes down
and the sky turns red,
it should get dark
but it's light instead.
I'm blinded by the headlights,
dazzled by the sight
of illuminated shop signs
shining in the night.
Oh, where has all the *dark* gone?
Give us back the night.
Even when I shut my eyes,
it's light, light, light.

C.J. Bennett

OVERNIGHT

Overnight,
While we slept,
The snow crept
Out of the sky
And blew its white breath
Over doorsteps and sills,
Gardens, fields and hills.
We woke to find
A world turned white
Overnight.

John Foster

WINTER MORNING

On my cold, cold toes
are some yellow socks

on the yellow socks
are some green, green boots

on the green, green boots
is a white, white sheet

on the white, white sheet
is a warm, warm rug

and the warm, warm rug
is red, red, red!

I can hear the rain
and it's time for school...

but I'd much rather stay
in BED, BED, BED!

Judith Nicholls

SARAH AND THE RED THINGS

'What can I have that's red?' asked Sarah one day at tea-time. 'Miss Munro wants us all to bring things to school for our Red Table.'

'How about a strawberry?' said Nana, who was spreading jam on some toast.

'It's the wrong time of the year for strawberries,' said Sarah's mummy.

'Someone would eat it anyway,' said Lucy, who was very fond of strawberries.

'What about your red socks?' suggested Sarah's daddy.

'No,' said Sarah, 'Miss Munro can't have those, because I want to wear them tomorrow, with the tartan skirt Nana gave me for my birthday.'

'It should be very easy to find something that's red,' said Mummy, 'because red is Sarah's favourite colour. There's your pillar-box money-box, for instance.'

'No good,' said Sarah. 'I need it to put my pocket money in because I'm saving up for a helicopter.'

'I know,' said Lucy, picking up the cat. 'You can take Jam Samwidge.'

The cat purred.

'He's not red,' said Sarah, stroking him behind the ears. 'He's orange. Besides, he's not allowed on tables!'

'Let's all close our eyes and think of all the red things we can,' said Daddy.

'All right,' said Sarah, closing her eyes. 'Jam tarts, traffic lights, my toothbrush and big London buses.'

'Newborn babies, clown's noses, sunsets and our front door,' said Mummy.

'Uncle Thomas's hair, Nana's car, chilli peppers and Irish Setters,' said Daddy.

'Red Riding Hood's hood, ketchup, ladybirds and Father Christmas,' said Lucy.

'Fire engines, my winter nightie, danger signs and Sarah's wellingtons,' said Nana.

They all opened their eyes.

'That's it,' said Mummy. 'She can take the wellingtons for the Red Table.'

'But I'm sure it's going to rain tomorrow,' said Sarah, 'and if it does I want to *wear* my wellingtons.'

'What are we to do?' said Daddy. 'Most of the red things we can think of are not the sort you can take to school, like our front door. And all the red things we *could* take are things that Sarah specially likes because red is her favourite colour.'

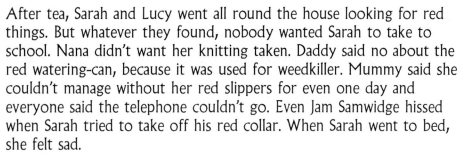

After tea, Sarah and Lucy went all round the house looking for red things. But whatever they found, nobody wanted Sarah to take to school. Nana didn't want her knitting taken. Daddy said no about the red watering-can, because it was used for weedkiller. Mummy said she couldn't manage without her red slippers for even one day and everyone said the telephone couldn't go. Even Jam Samwidge hissed when Sarah tried to take off his red collar. When Sarah went to bed, she felt sad.

'I don't want to be the only one without a red thing.'

In the morning, Sarah got dressed in her favourite red jumper, her new tartan skirt, her red socks and her wellington boots. Finally she put on the red wooden bracelet that Kathy gave her at her birthday party. But when it was time to go to school, she still didn't have anything to take to school for the Red Table.

'Pity about the front door,' said Mummy as she bumped Lucy down the steps in her buggy.

As usual, Sarah said hello to the snapdragons in the front garden, who said hello back to her when she pressed the sides of their faces. Then she noticed what colour they were!

'Mummy, can I take some snapdragons for the Red Table?'

'Of course,' said Mummy, and Sarah picked three crimson snapdragons.

'Take a tomato too,' said Mummy, 'not one that's still green or only orange.'

Sarah chose a really ripe tomato and then Mummy reached up and picked a spray of scarlet berries from the tree.

So when Sarah got to school, she had three things for the Red Table and she took them straight to Miss Munro. The Red Table was already quite full. There was a red scarf, a bright red rainhat, a shiny red ball for a christmas tree, a pot of strawberry jam, an Indian headdress made of red feathers and a glass jar with one red rose in it. Jamie had brought a bright red chilli pepper.

Miss Munro put Sarah's snapdragons and berries in with the rose and put the tomato on the table.

'I hope no-one eats it,' said Sarah.

'They'd better not try to eat the chilli!' said Jamie. 'It would burn their mouths.'

Miss Munro looked at Sarah in her red jumper, tartan skirt, socks and wellingtons.

'I see something else for our Red Table,' she said. Sarah felt a bit worried. Was it her red bracelet? She was sure that Kathy wouldn't want her to take it off. But the next minute, Miss Munro had cleared a big space on the table and she lifted *Sarah* up and put her on it.

'Come and see our Red Table now!' said Miss Munro and all the children came to look at Sarah.

From *Specially Sarah* by Mary Hoffman

Roy loved wearing hats. In fact, it was most unusual to see him without one. Whenever people saw him they said, 'Here comes Roy — and his hat.' And when they saw the hat he was wearing, 'Well I never — fancy that!'

Today Roy was feeling sad. He had been invited to a Yellow Party that afternoon, and this meant you had to wear as many yellow things as you could.

He had a yellow jumper and yellow socks and he wanted his yellow hat too — but he couldn't find it anywhere.

There was a knock on the door and his friend Sam asked, 'Would you like to come to the park with Mum and me?'

ROY, THE HAT BOY

Note to storyteller: The rhyme about Roy and his hat is repeated several times, and it is fun for the children/ child to join in each time it is repeated.

'No, thank you,' replied Roy.
'Why not,' asked Sam.
    'I've lost my yellow hat.'
    'Well, you've plenty of others,' replied Sam.
    'But I want my yellow one for the party.'
    His mother suggested that he went to the park whilst she had a really good look for his hat.
    'Oh, all right, but I must find a hat to wear,' said Roy, and he went off to his hat box.

He chose a black peaked one — then he could pretend he was in charge of the park. When he walked back into the room they all said,
    'Here comes Roy — and his hat.
    Well I never — fancy that!'
    He usually smiled back. But not today.
    On their way to the park they passed

quite a few other friends who all said,

'Here comes Roy – and his hat.

Well I never – fancy that!'

There were still no smiles from Roy – he was thinking about his yellow hat. It was one of his favourites; when he was wearing it, he felt very important. It was a digger driver's hat. His dad had been given it by a real digger driver and Roy wore it as often as he could.

When they reached the park, the man in charge looked at him and said,

'Here comes Roy – and his hat.

Well I never – fancy that!'

Roy was still unhappy. But then Sam's mum took out the football and for a while he forgot about his hat. He loved playing football with Sam and they ran and ran until they were both exhausted.

'Come on, you two,' called Sam's mum. 'Time to go home.'

'Just two more minutes,' said Sam, but Roy was ready to go when he'd been reminded of home.

'I wonder if Mum's found my yellow

hat?'

On the way back, the butcher came out of his shop to say good morning to Sam and his mum – but to Roy he said,

'Here comes Roy – and his hat.

Well I never – fancy that!'

Roy managed a small smile this time, because he had a feeling his mother would have found his hat.

As soon as he arrived home he asked her, 'Have you found my yellow hat?'

'I'm sorry, Roy,' she answered. 'I've hunted everywhere. I can't think what has happened to it.'

He almost cried then, but stopped when he heard a knock on the door and a voice call, 'Where's Roy, the Hat Boy?'

Roy recognised the barber's voice. He liked the barber because only yesterday when he'd finished cutting his hair he'd given him a new hat. It was made of cardboard with writing all over it.

He went to the door and the barber was holding the lost yellow hat.

'I think this must be yours. You were so eager to wear my hat home, you forgot this one.'

Roy jumped up and down with delight. He hugged his yellow hat to him and grinned at the barber.

'Thank you, thank you,' he said over and over again.

He went to the party that afternoon wearing his yellow socks and jumper *and* his yellow hat. When he walked in they all said,

'Here comes Roy – and his hat.

Well I never – fancy that!'

and Roy smiled an enormous smile!

From *What Shall We Do Today?* by Delphine Evans

PHOTOCOPIABLE RESOURCES

TAIL OF A PEACOCK

One morning, when Harry opened his eyes, he felt quite different. He didn't know why because his bedroom, and everything in it, was just the same and then he remembered. It was his birthday so no wonder he felt different. He had never been six years old before.

'Happy birthday,' said Mummy when Harry went downstairs to breakfast.

'Where are my presents?' said Harry.

'On the sitting-room table,' Mummy said. 'But breakfast first and presents after.'

'Happy birthday,' said Daddy who was already eating his.

'Egg,' said Susie who was sitting in her high chair and eating hers.

'Susie's got a new word,' Daddy said. 'Clever Susie.'

Susie didn't know many words yet because she wasn't even two, but she did know *Mummy* and *Daddy* and *Harry* and *shan't* and *mine* and *Snowdrop. Snowdrop* was her woolly rabbit. *Mine* was Susie's favourite word.

Breakfast didn't take long that day and then Harry ran into the sitting-room. He knew the two big presents were from Mummy and Daddy because they didn't have string and stamps, and the small parcels were from aunts and cousins because they did.

'Mine,' Susie said.

'It's Harry's birthday today and the presents are for Harry,' Mummy said. 'But I've got a new ribbon for Snowdrop.'

'No birthday. No, no, no,' Susie said and she flung Snowdrop on the floor and began to scream.

'*Birthday*, that's another new word,'

Mummy said, picking Susie up and cuddling her but Susie went on screaming.

Harry was opening his presents. The first big present was wrapped up in blue paper and sticky tape and inside was an Indian wigwam.

'Thanks. Magic,' Harry said and he put the wigwam up on the sitting-room floor and sat inside.

'Mine,' screamed Susie.

Harry took a long time to get the second big present undone because of Susie screaming. Inside was a feathery Indian head-dress with big red feathers and green feathers and yellow feathers.

'Thanks. Smashing,' Harry said and he put it straight on his head.

'Mine,' screamed Susie louder than ever. 'Mine, mine, mine.'

'Stop it,' said Harry. 'She's spoiling my birthday.'

'She's only small,' Mummy said. She had to shout rather because of Susie screaming. 'It's nearly time for school. You'd better open the other presents later.'

'All right,' said Harry and he put his biscuits in his pocket and Mummy put Susie in the pushchair and they set off down Small Street with Harry in his Indian head-dress.

'Who's this? Big Chief Sitting Bull?' the milkman said.

'It's me,' Harry said. 'It's my birthday.'

'No birthday,' hiccuped Susie. She had stopped screaming by this time but she was still rather pink.

'What lovely feathers! Happy birthday, Harry,' Mrs Robinson said when Harry went into school and everybody in Class One sang 'Happy Birthday' and then they

crowded round.

'I like the green feathers best,' Charlene said.

'Red good luck colour,' Tong said.

'Pretty,' said Moklissa, so softly that nobody heard.

It was a lovely day and after dinner Mrs Robinson took Class One out to the park with Sharon's mummy who helped on Friday afternoons.

In the park there was grass and trees and leafy bushes and lots of paths.

'Who wants to play rounders?' Mrs Robinson said and nearly everybody did but some people just sat on the grass by Sharon's mummy and baby George and watched.

Harry stood on the path. All along the edges there were feathers, not big, bright feathers like his Indian head-dress but small feathers from real birds. Feathers grey as a rainy day and feathers black as welly-boots and brown as earth and white as rice. Harry picked them up and wandered down the path with the bunch of feathers in his hand. He could still hear Class One but he couldn't see them because of the leafy bushes on either side.

Suddenly he saw the peacock. It had yellow eyes and blue-green feathers which shimmered in the sun like silk. Harry had never seen a peacock before and he stared and the peacock stared too because it had never seen a boy with red and green and yellow feathers on his head before. Then the peacock spread its long tail slowly into a big fan and turned round and round with all its tail feathers shaking and making a fluttery shuddery noise. *Shushy, shushy, shushy.*

'Magic,' said Harry and he turned round and round too, but he had to make the shushy noise with his mouth. Then he noticed something else, a blue-green tail feather lying on the grass just inside the pen. He could easily put his hand in and get

it but the peacock had such a sharp-looking beak.

Harry had eaten his biscuits at playtime but he found a few biscuit crumbs in the bottom of his pocket.

'Here you are,' he said and he dropped them on the grass and as the peacock pecked them up Harry reached in and got the feather, the beautiful blue-green tail feather which shimmered in the sun like silk.

'Oh, there you are,' said Mrs Robinson. 'You mustn't wander off like that or you might get lost.' But she wasn't really cross because it was his birthday.

'Real birds dropped all these feathers in the park,' Harry said, when Mummy came to fetch him after school with Susie in the pushchair. 'Could you sew them with the machine and make a real-bird feather head-dress for Susie?'

'Well, I think it would be easier to sew them by hand,' Mummy said and as soon as they got home that's what she did.

'Mine,' said Susie and she smiled when Mummy put the little feathery head-dress on her head with the beautiful peacock feather right in the front. 'Pretty.'

'That's another new word,' Harry said and after he had opened all his other presents he took his wigwam out to the garden and he and Susie played in it until it was time for tea.

'Who's this?' Daddy said when he came home.

'Big Chief Sitting Bull and Little Chief Sitting Calf,' Harry said.

'Little Chief Sitting Calf,' Susie said and that was six new words on Harry's birthday.

Clever Susie. Clever Harry.

From *Summer in Small Street* by Geraldine Kaye

UP ABOVE, DOWN BELOW

1. The sky is blue, the sky is blue, The sky is blue. High a-bove my head.

High a-bove my head, high a-bove my head. Blue sky high a-bove me, High a-bove my head.

2. The clouds are grey, the clouds are grey,
The clouds are grey, high above my head.
High above my head, high above my head
Clouds are grey above me,
High above my head.

3. The grass is green, the grass is green,
The grass is green, down beneath my feet.
Down beneath my feet, down beneath my feet
Green grass down below me,
Down beneath my feet.

4. The earth is brown, the earth is brown,
The earth is brown, down beneath my feet.
Down beneath my feet, down beneath my feet,
Brown earth down below me,
Down beneath my feet.

Ian Henderson-Begg

GREEN GREEN GREEN

Chorus

Green, green, green, Green's the world's fav-'rite col - our.

Green, green, green, Green is all___ a - round. *Fine (last time)*

1. Green is the grass, the leaves on the trees, The moss on the wall, The beans and the peas. *D.C.*

2. Green are the reeds that grow by the stream,
   Green are the insects that hate to be seen.

3. Green are the plants, they'll soon be in bloom
   To brighten the garden and drive out the gloom.

4. Green is the light that tells us to go
   Green is the colour you can't help but know.

Ian Henderson-Begg

CAN YOU TASTE THE COLOUR?

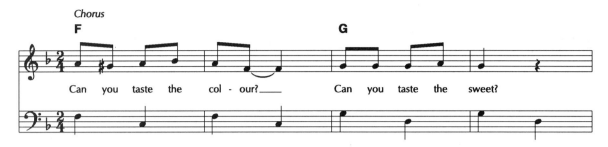

Chorus

Can you taste the col - our?___ Can you taste the sweet?

Can you taste the Smar - tie in our sweet - taste test - ing treat?

Each child then replies by testing a sweet and singing to the above 8 bars.

I can taste the colour,
I can taste the sweet,
I think it's a * _____ one *(*child says colour of sweet)*
In our sweet-taste testing treat.

Peter Morrell

COLOUR SPLASH

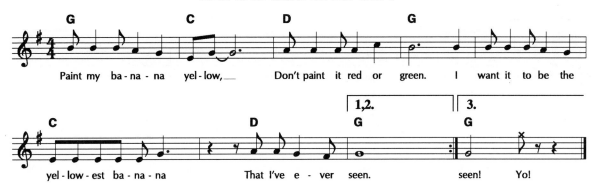

Paint my ba - na - na yel - low, ___ Don't paint it red or green. I want it to be the

1,2. **3.**

yel - low - est ba - na - na That I've e - ver seen. seen! Yo!

2. Paint my orange orange
Don't paint it red or green
I want it to be the orangest orange
That I've ever seen.

3. Paint my fingers purple
Don't paint them red or green
I want them to be the purplest fingers
That you've ever seen!

Ostinato: anything to shake or rattle or scrape to the following rhythm,

which could also be chanted:

1. Yel-low ba-na - na, yel-low ba - na - na.
2. O - ran - gy o - range, o - ran - gy o - range.
3. Pur - pl - est fin - gers, pur - pl - est fingers.

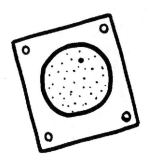

Words by Trevor Millum, music by Gill Parker

A CHAMELEON HAS NO STRIPES!

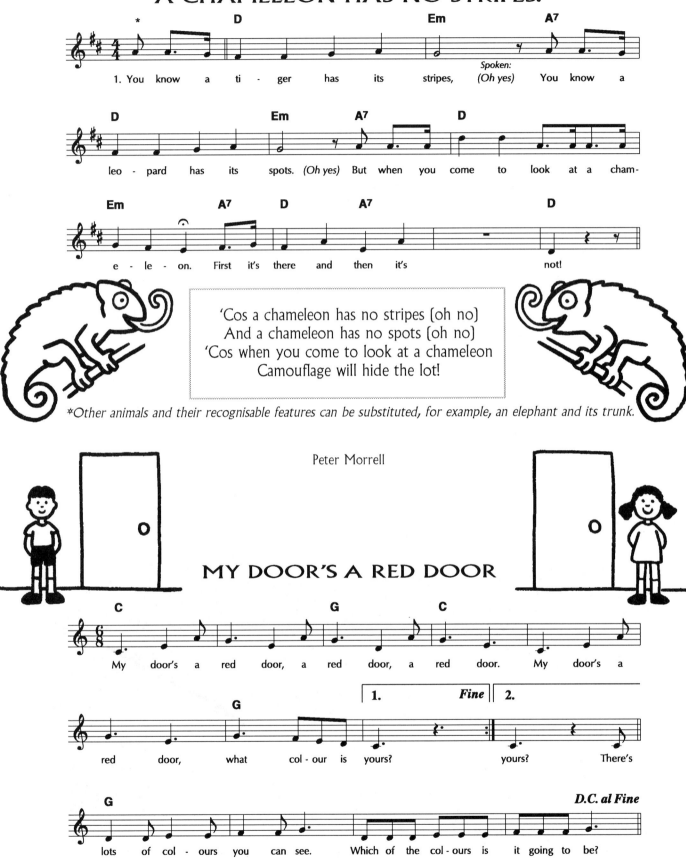

'Cos a chameleon has no stripes (oh no)
And a chameleon has no spots (oh no)
'Cos when you come to look at a chameleon
Camouflage will hide the lot!

Other animals and their recognisable features can be substituted, for example, an elephant and its trunk.

Peter Morrell

MY DOOR'S A RED DOOR

Clive Barnwell

BURN, CANDLE BURN

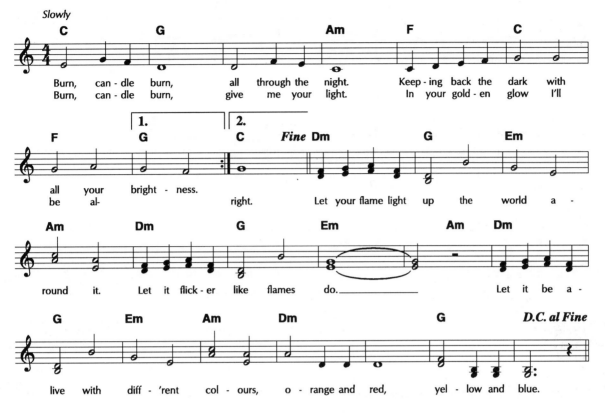

Slowly

Burn, can - dle burn, all through the night. Keep - ing back the dark with
Burn, can - dle burn, give me your light. In your gold - en glow I'll

all your bright - ness.
be al- right. Let your flame light up the world a -

round it. Let it flick - er like flames do._____ Let it be a -

live with diff - 'rent col - ours, o - range and red, yel - low and blue.

Clive Barnwell

MIDDLE OF THE RING

Quickly

What col-our did you wear to-day? What col-our did you wear to-day?

What col-our did you wear to-day? Have you got some red on? And

if you've got some red on, if you've got some red on,

if you've got some red on, move in-to the mid-dle of the ring.

A multi-purpose song which can be adapted: How did you get to school today? What shape can you find today? Miss out the note 'on' for single syllable words.

Instructions can vary, for example, What colour can you see today? Can you see a red thing? Go and find a red thing. Put it in the middle of the ring.

Children sing this sitting or standing in a circle.

Clive Barnwell

A RAINBOW WORLD

1. Red is the col-our that I wear, Red is the col-our ev-'ry-where, From the ber-ries bright to the ro-bin's breast, Red is the col-our I like best.

2. Orange is the colour that I wear, orange is the colour ev'rywhere,
From the Autumn leaves to the fruit on my plate,
Orange is the colour — it's just great!

3. Yellow is the colour that I wear, yellow is the colour ev'rywhere,
From the golden corn to the sun that shines,
Yellow is a colour that I like.

4. Green is the colour that I wear, green is the colour ev'rywhere,
From the tallest tree to the grass below,
Green is a colour that I know.

5. Blue is the colour that I wear, blue is the colour ev'rywhere,
From the deep blue sea to the sky up above,
Blue is a colour that I love.

6. Colours, colours that I wear, colours, colours, ev'rywhere,
God made them all to show that he cares,
A rainbow world for us to share.

Lesley Funge

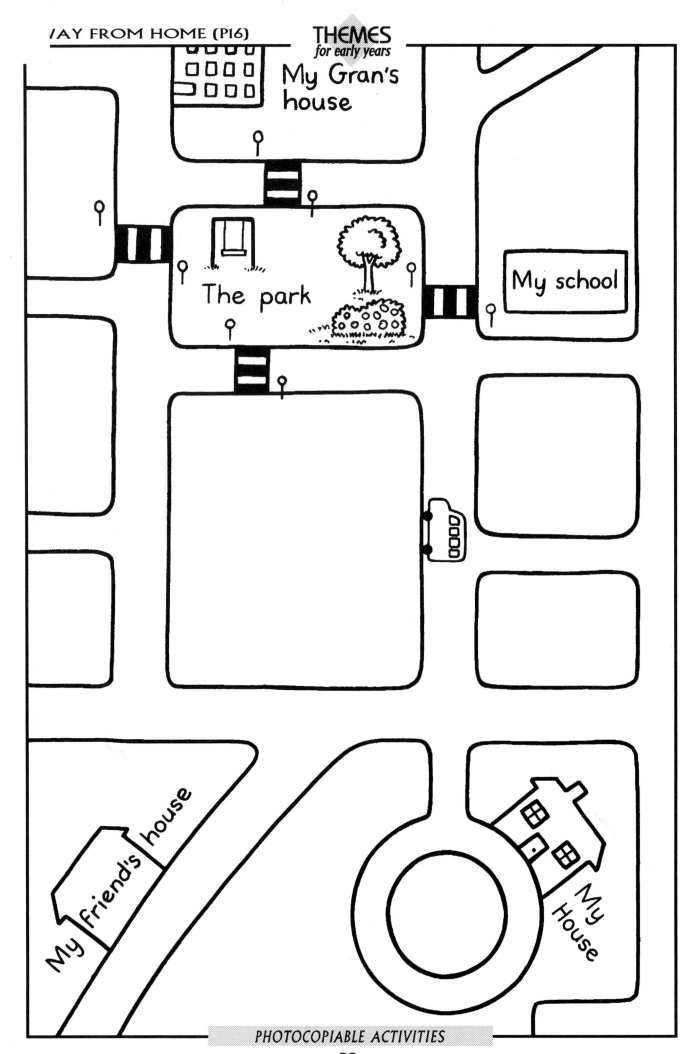

THEMES
for early years

My Gran's house

The park

My school

My friend's house

My House

THEMES
for early years

THEMES
for early years

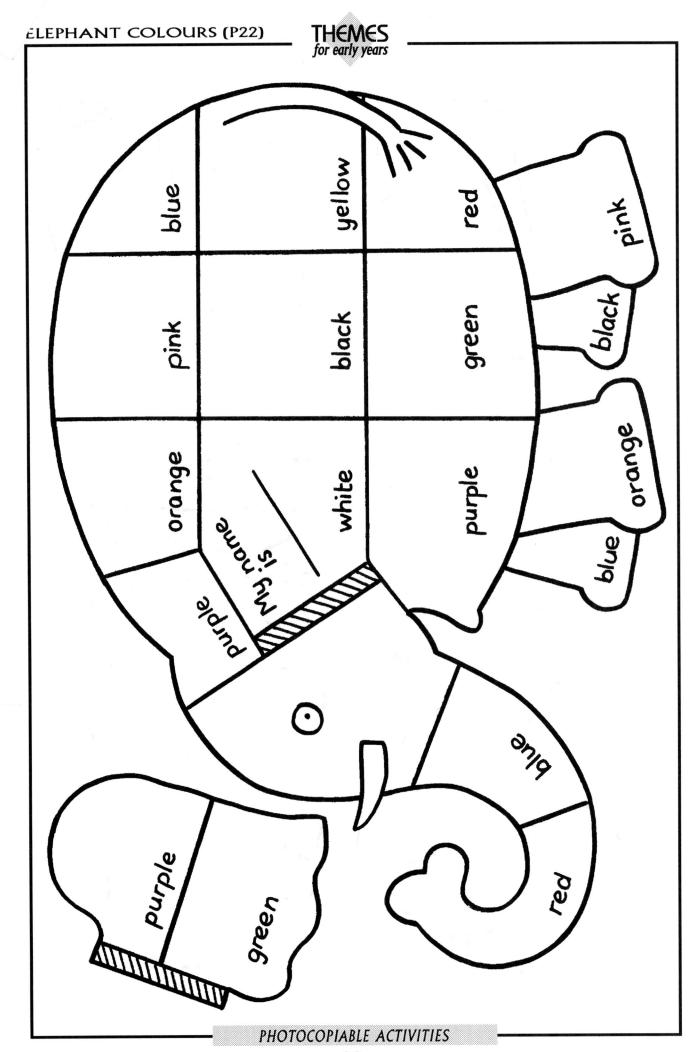

THEMES
for early years

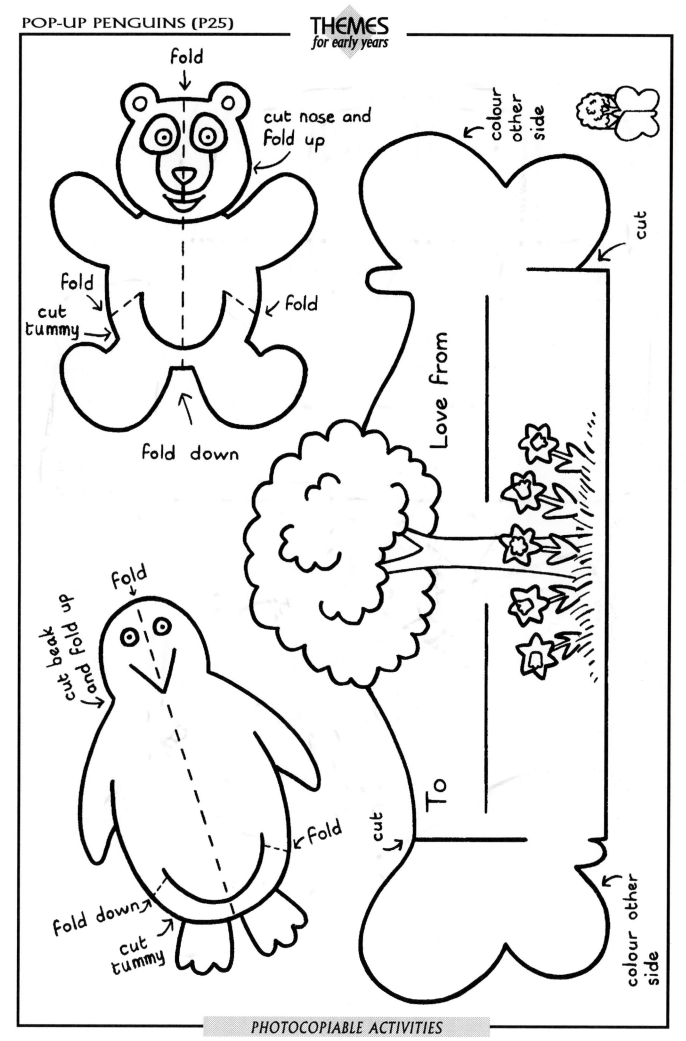

Fold

cut nose and
Fold up

colour
other
side

cut

fold
cut
tummy

fold

Love From

fold down

Fold

cut beak
and Fold up

fold

fold down
cut
tummy

cut

To

colour other
side

THEMES
for early years

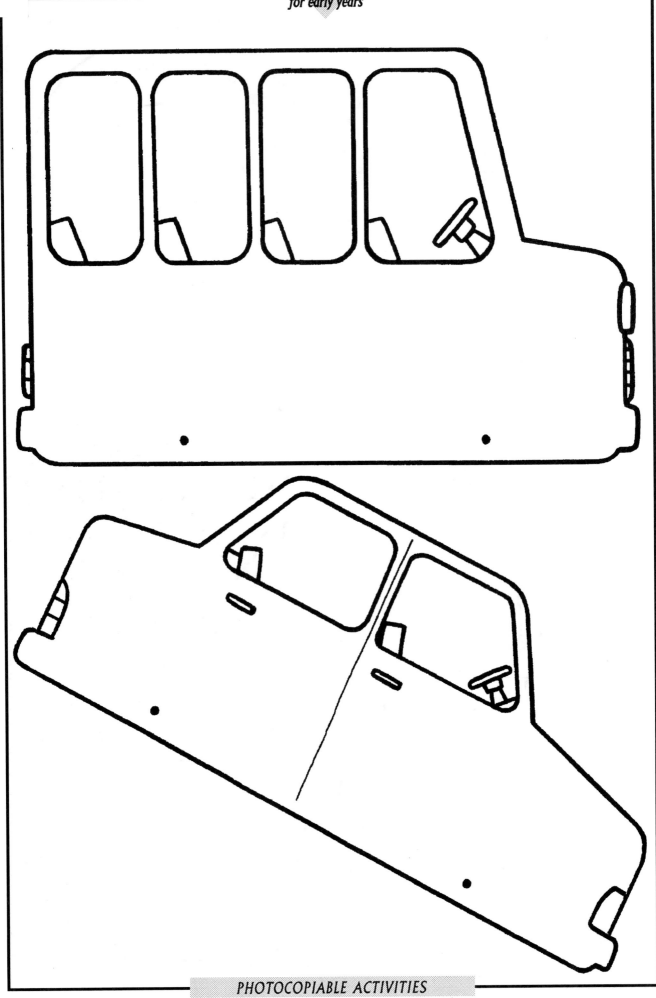

THEMES
for early years

THEMES
for early years

THEMES
for early years

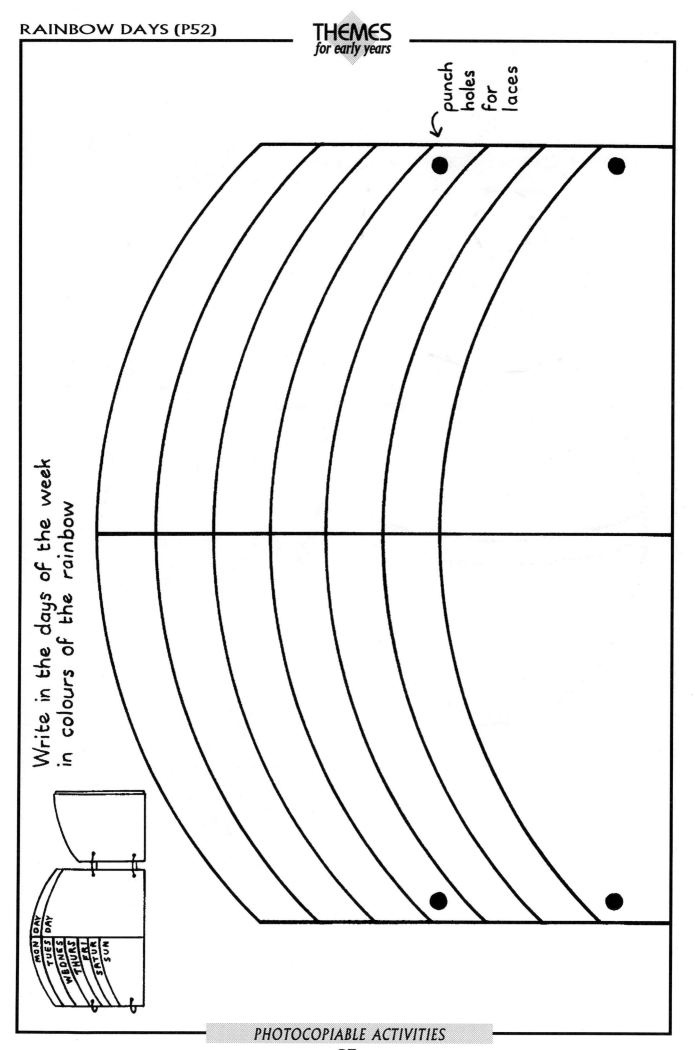

punch holes for laces

Write in the days of the week in colours of the rainbow

MON DAY
TUES DAY
WEDNES
THURS
FRI
SATUR
SUN

RECOMMENDED MATERIALS

STORIES AND INFORMATION BOOKS

The Big Alfie and Annie Rose Storybook, Shirley Hughes (Red Fox)
The Big Red Bus Ride, Peter Curry (Collins)
Child's Bible (Piccolo Books)
The Circus, Dick Bruna (Methuen)
Colour (MacDonald Starters)
Colours, Jan Pienkowski (Heinemann)
Colours and Shapes, Lynne Bradbury (Ladybird Books)
Colours Book, Angela Wilkes and Colin King (Usborne)
Colours of Things, Althea First Books (Dinosaur Publishing Ltd)
The Elephant and the Bad Baby, Elfrida Vipont and Raymond Briggs (Puffin)
Elmer, David McKee (Red Fox)
Green Eggs and Ham, Dr. Seuss (Collins)
How to Hide a Butterfly and Other Insects, Ruth Heller (Kingfisher Books)
I Don't Want to, Sally Grindley (Methuen)
Just-So Stories, Rudyard Kipling (picture book version) (Alfred Knopf Publishers)
Kipper's Birthday, Mick Inkpen (Hodder & Stoughton)
Knowabout Pattern, Henry Pluckrose (Watts)
The Ladybird Bible Story Book (Ladybird Books)
Mary Poppins, P.L. Travers (Penguin)
Mister Benn, Red Knight (for older children), David McKee (Picture Puffin)
Mr Rabbit and the Lovely Present, Charlotte Zolotow (Picture Lions)
The Mixed-up Chameleon, Eric Carle (Puffin)
Mouse Paint, Ellen Stoll Walsh (Orchard Books)
Moving Molly, Shirley Hughes (Red Fox)
My First Book of Colours (series in English, Gujarati, Chinese, etc.) (Mantra Publishing)
My Little Book of Colours, Jan Ormerod (Walker Books)
My Naughty Little Sister, Dorothy Edwards (Mammoth)
My Science Book of Colour, Neil Ardley (Dorling Kindersley)
Now We are Six, A.A. Milne (Methuen)
Spot Goes to the Circus, Eric Hill (Picture Puffin)
Tall Inside, Jean Richardson (Picture Puffin)
Tom and Pippo See the Moon, Helen Oxenbury (Walker Books)
The Very Hungry Caterpillar, Eric Carle (Picture Puffin)
When My Naughty Little Sister Was Good, Dorothy Edwards (Mammoth)
When We Were Very Young, A. A. Milne (Methuen)
Where the Wild Things Are, Maurice Sendak (Picture Lions)
Who Said Red?, Mary Serfozo (Picture Lions)

SONG BOOKS

Apusskidu: Songs for Children (A & C Black)
Bright Ideas for Early Years: Action Rhymes and Games; Science Activities; Sharing Time and Assemblies, Max de Boo (Scholastic)
Okki-Tokki-Unga: Action Songs for Children (A & C Black)
Sing a song, One (Nelson)
Someone's Singing, Lord (A & C Black)
Songs, Scholastic Collections (Scholastic)

OTHER RESOURCES

Roamer (Valiant Technology Limited). From NES Arnold, Ludlow Hill Road, West Bridgford, Nottingham NG2 6HD.

Teddy Bear Colour Match Express. Jigsaw-type puzzle with 24 train trucks in six bright colours which are matched with 24 teddy bear passengers. Available from Step by Step Ltd, Lavenham Road, Beeches Trading Estate, Yate, Bristol BS17 5QX.

Colour and Shape Lotto. A matching game with a variety of shapes and colours. From NES Arnold (address above).

Colour Match-ups. Picture cards which have holes for colours. A Ravensburger game available from NES Arnold (address above).

Bucket of Beads. 240 plastic beads of six different shapes in five colours, stored in a resealable bucket. The set comes with four threading laces. From Step by Step Ltd (address above).